# They
# CALL ME
# MZEE

## ONE MAN'S SAFARI INTO BRIGHTEST AFRICA

# LEE B. MULDER

ISBN: 1463741049
ISBN-13: 9781463741044


CreateSpace, North Charleston, SC

# Dedication

To Sonia, Will and Emily,
   the ones who watched me go
    and wondered at the dad they welcomed back

# Acknowledgements

I want to express my sincere thanks to everyone mentioned by name in this book. Only a few names have been changed for privacy purposes but you will know who you are. The information, the conversations, the insight and the life stories you shared without hesitation were a joy to receive; each of them became an indelible stitch in the fabric of this work. I especially want to thank Prof. Emmanuel Tumusiimwe-Mutebile and his wife Betty who provided vital food, housing and encouragement during the initial grueling 10 days of interviews in Kampala.

Most of all, I want to thank Rev. Dr. Ben Tumuheirwe, my pastor, my friend and the visionary who invited me and so many others to simply "come home" to Uganda. For this work, Ben worked tirelessly providing access to people in Uganda who had been touched by the AIDS crisis – officials, acquaintances in government, church, village and family that I as an outsider simply would never have been to achieve in a lifetime. Working with *Owesheimwe* Ben over the years, I have been privileged to share the lives of many, many Ugandans and, in turn, become a tiny part of their history by living it with them.

# Table of Contents:

## Part I: Going Home

## Part II: The Reality of AIDS

## Part III: Up Country

## Part IV: Journal Notes

# Introduction

This is the story of one country in Africa. There are 61 sovereign states and territories situated on or near the continent and each has its own story, but this one is exceptional, a surprise.

If you count from the day the government was wrested from the control of idiot dictators in 1986, the Republic of Uganda, East Africa is only slightly more than two decades old. As a region, however, people have lived in this part of the Great Rift Valley since the beginning of mankind, developing an orderly society of tribes and villages, culture and skills, trade and warfare.

Its modern story is one of a people who, over the last 120 years, have endured Colonialism, corrupt leadership, famine, disorganization, rebellion, disease, the Sexual Revolution, the Cold War, the UN and warring neighbors, to become a productive nation of faith and enterprise. It is the story of how this one nation has become the world's shining example of how to deal with the AIDS pandemic. It is also my story, a personal journey, one man's intimate venture into another culture and an unexpected safari into faith.

My journey to Uganda began in the front pew of a Presbyterian church shortly before the turn of the century. I was not sitting there, of course. I was with most of the other people toward the back. But during the service, I could not help but notice this fellow in front, a black man in a congregation of white faces. He raised his hands high when he prayed, like a weed growing out of a field of people clinging to their programs. He swayed and bounced during the music. And during one particularly lively 18th century tune, he jumped. Off the ground. More than once. He clapped his hands above his head in time to the music and he smiled a radiant smile toward heaven when he was listening to God's word. I had never seen such joy in worship.

At that time, I was part of the church's missions committee and so was not surprised when the senior pastor brought this fellow over to me after the service. "You need to meet Ben," was all he said. In front of me was a not-so-tall, broad-shouldered African man with bright eyes and a luminescent grin. "I am Ben from Uganda," he said. I shook his hand in welcome, not having the slightest idea where in Africa Uganda was situated.

Comments about "the jumping man" murmured through the church for the next week. People wondered who he was. How did he find his way to our church in white bread suburbia? What did he want? This was before Philip Jenkins' *The Next Christendom* would enlighten people in the West (Europe and America) of the oncoming revival of Christian joy and belief coming from the South (South America, Asia and Africa). We had no idea we were about to be evangelized or even that we needed to be.

Some time passed before I would see Ben again, but again, it was in church.

In 2001, our African visitor shepherded a group of American teens to Uganda, including one young man from our church. When they returned, our teenager was invited to take five minutes during Sunday worship to give his testimony of how the trip had affected him. He had a ponytail. His skin was ravaged by acne. But he was no longer the shy, nerdy, seemingly lost boy I had known. In bold tones and clear language, he spoke about the people of Uganda who, simply by including our young people in their daily lives, had reconfigured his perception of faith and had forever changed his idea of what it meant to be a follower of Christ. The young man's finale was to invite his fellow teen travelers to the front of the congregation to perform a native Ugandan dance, much like the jumping for joy I had witnessed of Ben that first time. And there was Ben, beating the drum for them.

Over the next few years, I grew close to Ben Tumuheirwe and his family while he completed his studies at Trinity International University and his wife, Lilian, earned a degree in fashion and drapery design at the local college. I babysat their children. I put up towel racks in their bathroom. I met other Americans who were enchanted by this man, had felt his magnetism, wanted to support him in his work, and I realized I was not alone in having those sensations. I attended Ben's ordination as an Anglican Priest. I helped write a grant so our church could hire him as "Missionary in Residence" in order that he could complete the class work for his doctorate degree. In 2003, I finally accepted Ben's persistent invitation and traveled with him and nine others from my church to his home country.

I confess I went to Uganda not as an evangelist or a missionary but as a traveler curious to see the place. The journalist in me wanted to discover the truth about AIDS in Africa firsthand. I wanted to see the Sally Struthers children with fly-blown faces, babies with bloated bellies, the emaciated dead lying in the gutters. I wanted to duck the bullets of wild-eyed rebels and walk among the throngs of withering refugees. I wanted to taste the anti-American venom of Mogadishu, see the blood-stained streets of Idi Amin, touch the squalor of apartheid, smell the fear of brutal tribal war of Rwanda, feel the blind, government-fueled hatred of white citizens displaced by the impoverished blacks of Zimbabwe and witness the ostentatious results of blatant thievery of public funds by President Monarchs driving Rolls Royces.

Imagine my surprise when I found none of these.

I know there are many people dying of HIV/AIDS in Uganda, but in many years of traveling in towns, back roads and dingy neighborhoods, I saw only one case. There is poverty which, in Africa, has a completely different context than in any country in the first world. There is government corruption here, less so than in the Latin American countries I have visited and perhaps only slightly more insidious than that in the U.S. There was rebel activity in the North – a 20 year-old skirmish that ended in 2006. But these were not the things that consumed Ugandans in their daily life.

Instead I found a large capitol city with glass skyscrapers, buzzing with vehicles, where people did not fear strolling at night. The population is mostly lean and healthy, fed on a diet of organically grown fruits and vegetables and kept strong by hard physical labor. I found a large and growing, highly educated and productive middle class. I found pride. I found enterprise. I found inordinately kind hospitality with smiling, polite children and warm, welcoming adults. I found a beautiful place with snow-capped mountains and pristine lakes, breathtaking views, savannahs and national parks full of wild animals. I found an unbounded sense of humor. I met people who were proud of their national leaders and I met national leaders who genuinely care about making life better for their people. And I found children. Scores and scores and scores of children.

The outward scars of Idi Amin's reign are all gone. Private enterprises stolen by his government in the 1970s have long since been returned to their owners. The animals, once slaughtered to the point of extinction in the national parks, are plentiful. Entebbe airport, forever in our memory as the scene of an Israeli attack to free people in a highjacked airliner in 1976, is modern and efficient. The barracks where political prisoners were tortured and killed have been turned into schools. The last burned-out hulk of a tank sitting by the side of the road has been removed.

I witnessed the results of what happens when an entire generation of people including more than a million parents dies of HIV/AIDS, leaving their children to fend for themselves. I saw the child-headed families in the dumps and the fields or as clumps of glassy-eyed waifs in castoff clothing worn ragged and filthy, just staring into space. The AIDS orphans were everywhere. They broke our hearts and inspired us to action, but they did not beg. To these children, the threat was not AIDS, but starvation, malaria, tuberculosis, dysentery or predatory adults.

Taken altogether, I found a nation of people who have far less material wealth than people in the West and who, by comparison, may be called poor but who, in fact, do not feel, live, or act poor. They live every day working hard. Many earn the equivalent of one U.S. dollar in order to survive one more day, but here is the mystery: they do it with joy in their hearts, thanking God as they go. With little else in their lives, they consider having faith in God as vital to their lives as air, food and water. I had found brightest Africa and it changed me forever.

*Mzee Lee Twesigye, Chicago, 2011*

PS: This is book is written from the point of view of an American not raised in poverty. Throughout the report I have worked to be accurate about my perceptions of the Ugandan culture as well as my own Western reactions to things. I'm sure the Ugandans will view many of my assessments differently, probably laughing all the way, but hopefully the reader will gain insight into both the differences between our cultures and our similarities as well. The reporting is mine alone; if your experience in Uganda has been different, I would love to hear it.

**Mzee** – (muh-ZAY) (noun) –
1. (Luganda) Respected elder, father or patriarch
2. (Swahili)  Dottering old coot

# PART I
## Going Home

*"If you understand the beginning well,*
*the end will not trouble you."*

- *African Proverb*

# Arrivals

*"Gosh Toto, we're Not in Kansas Anymore."*
- Dorothy, *The Wizard of Oz*

I step from the airplane at Entebbe Airport and find Lake Victoria lying still in the muggy dawn, scribing a perfect line on the horizon. The air is sweet and thick, pungent with the smell of grasses and lakeside muck. There is no sound other than footsteps on the aluminum jetway stairs.

Smartly uniformed attendants guide us into the airport building. We enter, having no idea where to go. There are six booths for returning nationals and those with visas but we visitors who planned to buy visas at the airport are directed to wait in line at a single door in the corner. It takes some time to reach the office, our first exposure to African Time. Entering the tiny room where two uniformed officials sit behind desks, each passenger hands over $30.00 American and a passport. The desks are covered with cash; if someone produces a $50.00 bill, the clerk swirls the pile around awhile until two tens appear for change. A thin young man, sleepy-faced, wearing a frayed shirt and a skinny tie holds my passport and sweeps some cash out of the way so he can fill out a yellow piece of paper with a lot of blanks.  He asks automatically "How long will you be staying?"

"Two weeks," I reply.

"You could stay longer," he says quietly. "A year maybe?" He has a twinkle in his eye.

"I would like that."

"I also," he says, with a smile and a nod.  He stamps my passport with a tribal crest. "Welcome to Uganda."

Our baggage comes round the carousel.  People load the free carts.  Following our host and mission team leader Ben Tumuheirwe, our carts piled high with donated goods and imported equipment, we wind our way through the "nothing to declare" lane and past the final doors.   Suddenly we are surrounded by song because Ben is in the bear hug of a tall man in a New York Jets tee shirt.  The two are singing something African "... *omolokozee.*" A slapping high-five. A loud, laughing exchange in some African lingo.  Everyone in the arrivals lounge is smiling now.  A grinning Ben introduces us to his best friend Denis and leads us to the parking lot where ten dozen weaverbirds are chattering in the dawn, fluttering as they build upside down nests in a leafless tree overhead.  We have two vans, one for luggage and one for people, both too small for their loads but we do not care because we are no longer on an airplane and our feet are on African soil.

As we leave the airport, the first thing I see is the fire-gutted skeleton of a dead airliner lying in the grass, a backdrop for a boy tending goats. The second thing I see is the United Nations staging area with two enormous cargo jets and a hundred new SUVs aligned like dominoes next to stacks and stacks of cargo containers, each one painted virginal white with a large black U-N on it.  Later I will learn Entebbe Airport is the central

U.N. logistics center for the Great Lakes Region. There are signs for resorts, a thirsty-looking golf course, squatty office buildings, a gated government complex and soon we are driving on the wrong side of the road, British-style. It is barely past dawn but people are hard at work, the women carrying loads on their heads and babies on their backs. Men on bicycles deliver milk. Gas at the local Shell station is posted at 1800 shillings per liter (about $6.00 /gallon). The land is covered with a fine red soil the color of cinnabar.

Soon, the hills of Kampala loom in the distance.

As we enter the city on Queen's Way, my first impression is chaos. The traffic here is an impossibly roiling, bubbling stew of cars, trucks, bicycles, pedestrians, hawkers with toys, hawkers with newspapers, hawkers with oranges, motorcycles with and without passengers, cows, chickens and goats, all in perpetual motion only just barely not colliding and all perfectly normal. "Yipes." I jump. Riding shotgun, I want to tell Denis, "You just missed that guy by a half inch," but I don't because it just happened again. Everything with wheels is Japanese. Pickup trucks carry the names "tsubis," "oyot" "issa" on the tailgates because government-required reflectors cover the end letters of the vehicle logos. Taxi vans called *matatus* cruise the streets with the side doors open, a conductor hawking for passengers as the vehicle cruises through traffic. A sign on the back says "14 passengers maximum" but there are at least 20 inside with the conductor hawking for more. As we creep our way down the boulevard, our car windows are open and, only inches away, the windows of a *matatu* are open. I quietly wish the woman in the smart teal suit sitting there good day. She nods and smiles in return.

The city is dense with signs, with vehicles, with sounds, with strange aromas, with people everywhere. For me, it was uncomfortable coming from the Land of Open Spaces and a Culture of Self to be dropped into this hive, this swirling mass of busy-looking people hurrying with purposeful walks and serious looks on their faces. I would see many parts of Kampala in the days and years to come and the scene never changed or even slowed down. Everywhere there were always masses of people. The taxi park, a maggoty city unto itself with thousands of cars waiting for passengers. The roadside markets jammed with humanity at midnight, throngs at universities, clusters of motorcycle taxis called *boda bodas* on every corner. I could only imagine that, growing up in large families in cramped spaces, children sleeping in piles like puppies, ten to twelve people to a room, a person would regard these crowds as normal, would actually take comfort in the close proximity and the constant rubbing of others. But it gave me the creeps. I know why. I come from Chicago where, from an early age, I have been conditioned to believe black-skinned people gathering in groups usually means trouble. But I'm not in Chicago, am I? In fact, here, I am the minority and I quickly learn there is nothing to fear.

We work our way between and around Kampala's seven hills to a polyglot neighborhood of shops and huts and a market with everything for sale from banana leaves to blank DVDs to luggage to dresses on white mannequins to eucalyptus poles to big stalks of green bananas. Little home-made kiosks advertise "Air Time" or "Phone Recharge." A sign points to the TeleTubbies pre-school. Goats are tethered to trees. Pigs and chickens roam the backyards. Shops are made of half-containers or truck bodies supported by logs or rocks. The dusty red-clay road we are on has jagged ruts two feet deep. A narrow side road near the market is flanked by rain gutters four feet deep and there are no guard rails. We split off onto another side road where the car creeps across eroded canyons but even at slow speed the passengers inside are tossed about until, at last, we reach our host's home. Denis honks. A reinforced steel gate topped by sharp spikes slides open. "You are welcome," he says even though we haven't thanked him yet. What he means is "You are welcome to my home." Now, at mid-morning, it is quiet in his spacious house amid palm trees and frangipani and the sun is strong. The colors are vibrant. Thick steel burglar bars cover the windows and doors. The view out the back, over the lawn, is a brick-making operation in someone's back yard. Nonetheless, a simple breakfast of bread, hard-boiled eggs and fresh sweet pineapple, tea and Nescafe is waiting for us. We are home.

Americans generally know little or nothing of Africa. The information we have has been doled out in tiny fabricated scraps of media: The movies: *Hotel Rwanda, Blood Diamond, Tears of the Sun, The Last King of Scotland*, the horrific stories of HIV/AIDS, the dubiously altruistic publicity stunts of rock stars or movie actors. The shocking 2003 documentary *Invisible Children* has been shown in over 1,000 high schools is still creating sympathy and taking donations for a conflict that ended in 2006. By now, most people know Oprah Winfrey opened a school for girls in South Africa. Few people understand why. Many have griped to her, "Why would you do that for those children and not the poor in our country?" Oprah gets it. Her reply? "You ain't seen poor 'til you've been there, honey."

Most Americans have no sense of geography about Africa. They may have heard about Sudan but few have looked for it on a map. South Africa is easy: it's south. Other than that, ask any high school student in America to describe the location of Ghana or Niger, Cameroon, Ethiopia, Malawi or Burundi and 999 times out of a thousand, you'll most likely get the universal answer, "Whatever."

"Oh, I've always wanted to go to Africa," someone says. "What part," I query. "Oh, you know, Africa." Or someone says, "I hear you've been to Africa. How was it?" I reply, "I've really only been to Uganda." "Really?" is the reply. "Where's that?"

Yet, based on little or no real information, we still have our stereotypes. "Everybody is dying of AIDS. You can get gunned down by in the streets by rebel armies with automatic weapons. Everybody is dirt poor." Thus it is a shock for visiting Westerners to find vibrant cities bursting with activity, luxury hotels, glittering skyscrapers, universities packed with students, well-dressed business people hurrying about their business and a wide variety of delicious food in markets and restaurants. In the capital city of Uganda there are history museums, shopping malls, theaters, a sports stadium and a zoo. We see no sick or dying people lying in the gutters – we are told we must go to the hospital or the slums to find them. There may be a guy with a gun in the lobby of a bank and truckloads of uniformed security guards swarming out at dusk like bats from a cave to protect property from the pilferers, but we see no armies bullying the population. Business people in neckties pack the restaurants. Mercedes Benz, BMW and high-end Mitsubishi Pajeros are common. There's a food court with pizza, fried chicken and a Panera-like fast-food bakery. What's not to like?

Now that I've been to Uganda multiple times, it is great sport to watch Americans come here for the first time because it forces me to remember my own introduction to this culture. No matter how well we have been briefed, no matter how many photos we have seen, websites visited, orientations attended, videos viewed, or stories heard, the reality of the place puts every single first-time visitor on sensory overload within hours just as it did to me. It is no wonder, for how can people compute such a difference between expectations and reality in a whole new world without a bit of a shock? It takes some time to realize all the young children have very short hair which makes it is difficult to tell boys from girls. Why? There is little money for hair care products. It is a surprise when little girls in perfectly white pinafores curtsey when they meet you or a young house helper kneels to present a fork for your meal. It is pure joy and surprise to go to church amidst singing and dancing and jumping and find yourself clapping and dancing as well. One man told me, "I was in Uganda for only a day before I ran out of categories, you know, those places where we store things in our mind for future retrieval. I just didn't know where to put the things my senses were taking in."

Everyone has his or her assimilation process. One group from Mississippi was so wary while in Uganda, they wouldn't touch the local food. Fresh fruit is like candy here, but they wouldn't sample it, fearing dreadful diseases, opting instead for meals of power bars. They drank bottled water, of course, but were afraid to come in contact with tap or well water, and so they bathed with bottled water as well. As a group, they exuded an ever-present scent of Purel™. It is sad to come so far and experience so little, but it also speaks to the fear we Americans have of those things lurking outside our comfort zones. This was not the case for an American pastor who hopped out of the car at a town full of street vendors and bought sizzling meat sticks off the hibachi from a grandma and a bottle of water from a little girl in a gingham dress. Standing there, white-skinned, bearded, in a Hawaiian shirt, he just munched away while the throngs of people stared and smiled and shook their heads.

Most people assimilate the change slowly, taking it as it comes. Group dynamics being what they are, every once in awhile, someone will say, "Look at that!" Heads swing to look and, as they days wear on, each person is busy sorting through his or her own discoveries, slowly morphing as cracks appear in our preconceptions, or hanging on as the car swerves to miss a pothole. These things are so foreign to our limited lives, like Dorothy dropped into the land of Oz, someone eventually says it: "Well, Toto, we're not in Kansas anymore."

I have seen many facets of Kampala life: At a tiny house reached somewhere deep inside a maze of streets where we must walk a plank across the storm gutter to get to the front door, the owner who has offered us accommodation apologizes for the size of the house, but says proudly, "It may be small, but it's all mine." The Baha'i Temple, the only one on the continent of Africa, seen in the distance from Ben's front porch, sits quietly majestic atop a hill of manicured gardens, its golden dome shining in the equatorial morning light. If it's Friday, legions of people dressed in flawless white from head to toe emerge from the cardboard slums to go to mosque. At a raggedy school with paint peeling from the walls, the students are diligently writing with stubs of pencils. Densely packed squatter communities made of odd board and scrap metal shacks are overhung by a haze of wood smoke. Sturdy brick homes are surrounded by tall walls topped with broken glass. There are apartment blocks akin to Communist-era East Berlin along main avenues not far from luxury hotels like the Colonial, the Sheraton, the Serena and the Speke which feature stone lobbies, gleaming bars and uniformed doormen. If you enter Kampala on the side roads at Mukono, you'll pass under a grove of orange and avocado trees. Drive a mile more and you'll find dingy, mud-walled inns; a mile further and you're surrounded by high-walled mansions on Kololo Hill.

One of the homes on Kololo belongs to the Governor of the Bank of Uganda, the equivalent of Alan Greenspan or whoever happens to be the head of the U.S. Federal Reserve Bank. The largest number I ever saw on a check hangs on a wall in this house on the hill. In the mid-1990s, the Governor became something of a legend in the annals of modern African development when he negotiated a loan for $1 billion from the World Bank to pay for a new program of free public education being pioneered by the nation's President. The bank paid in Ugandan shillings which, at the time, were being exchanged at the rate of 1,700 shillings to the dollar, making the amount on the check  1,700,000,000,000 shillings – that's one point seven *trillion*.

A blowup of that check is framed and hanging on the wall of his house. The first question that ran through my mind when I saw it was "how many checks has the World Bank written with this many zeros?" The second question was, "What happened to the money?"

To answer those questions, I must introduce you to Emmanuel Tumusiimwe-Mutebile, the Governor, and his wife Betty.

The Governor is described as "a hulking, hard-drinking hammer of a person, the chief architect of Uganda's success story and the greatest contributor to Africa's struggle against poverty in his generation" – all in the same sentence by author Sebastian Mallaby in his book *The World's Banker*.[1]

Mallaby reports that Gov. Mutebile grew up poor, the son of a school cook. As a student leader in the early 1970s he stood up and denounced Idi Amin's expulsion of Uganda's Asians, risking his life has he did so. He fled Uganda in disguise and was lucky enough to meet British economist Walter Elkan in Kenya who was impressed enough by the young man to arrange for Mutebile to study under him Durham University. Mutebile graduated to Balliol College, Oxford and then, in the late 1970s, moved to Tanzania, a center for Ugandan exiles. Also in Tanzania at this time was a young activist named Yoweri Museveni who was destined to oust the last dictator and re-establish a parliamentary government in Uganda in 1986. When his army overthrew Milton Obote, Museveni found Mutebile already in place as the country's leading financial technocrat.

Tumusiimwe means "Let us give Him thanks" in the Governor's native language and Mallaby is effusive about the influence this one man has had on shaping a productive government in Africa. Early on in the Museveni government, Mutebile drew up a pro-market economic plan that could move the country forward. By the mid-1990s, he had taken a chaotic mess of a bureaucracy and created a machine that could drive good policy forward, often with the help of major

---

1    Mallaby, Sebastian, *The World's Banker*, Penguin Press, 2004, p. 219

donors such as the World Bank. Within his own office, Mutebile always had a team of young British economists working for him even though Ugandan colleagues chided him about opening up the ministry to foreigners. The Governor laughed at them. "What are they going to do here, walk off with the furniture?" It was in Uganda's national interest to harness these hard-working outsiders whose salaries were paid by the World Bank and other donors because, alongside them he was training a new cadre of Ugandan technocrats in order to build a competent government.

Until the 1990s, Mallaby writes, Uganda had no real budget process. The government made promises and spent money in all directions without any real sense of where it came from. By 1992, inflation hit an annualized rate of 200 percent. But putting solid data collection and budgeting procedures in place tamed the inflation beast. Within a few years Uganda was transformed from a place where there was no hope of implementing good policy to a place where smart ideas could make a difference. The tamed beast could now attract investment capital. By 1996, The World Bank was convinced its investment in Uganda for Universal Public Education was well-placed.[2]

Today, the Governor lives the life of a major corporate CEO. Besides being Governor of the Bank of Uganda he is the Permanent Minister of Finance which means he cannot be removed from office by either the President or the Parliament. He has virtually unlimited resources and is responsible for thousands of employees. The Governor and his wife Betty live in a home they have added to over the years which now includes separate buildings for guests, a swimming pool and a terrace large enough to hold a reception for 100 people. His

2    Ibid, pp. 220-222

neighbors on Kololo are embassies, sons of potentates and African entrepreneurs. Mutebile is chauffeured around in a gunmetal gray Mercedes Benz with heavily tinted windows. His house is under 24-hour guard by bored looking young men carrying machine guns. He and his wife travel the world. They own a farm and a dairy and a second home on an island in Lake Bunyonyi where his is the only pleasure yacht on the lake. She has a retail business in Kampala and is an accomplished interior designer.

The first time I went to Mutebile's house, I was in astounded at the prosperity. I supposed that truly powerful people need to create a powerful personal atmosphere to deal with other powerful people, but this was clearly the good side of town. Just driving up Kololo Hill, getting glimpses of massive estates with addresses called "plots" with tile roofs and terraces behind high walls and solid gates, rising, ever rising, the fork to the left, ever higher. I had a brief recollection of Al Capone who had an office at 35 E. Wacker Drive in Chicago, in the dome of the tallest building in town, with windows on all sides so nobody could sneak up on him. I concluded that these are the Ugandan equivalent of castles built of stone on impassible peaks in Bavaria.

We had spent the day visiting schools in the back alleys of Kampala where kids in raggedy clothes played in the filthy gutters. Driving here we passed the markets, teeming in the night with people, many nourished by old women sitting in the dirt, tending their charcoal cookers, selling food for a few shillings to some of the throng. Now we would be treated to a light buffet on white table cloths on the terrace under the stars of the Southern Cross, overlooking the seven hills with twinkling city lights, the haze of wood smoke, and the invisible mass of people in perpetual motion below us.

Over the course of the conversation, I learned that the trillion shillings went for public education as promised. "We accomplished what no one ever thought could be done," Mutebile said. "The program was created to make free public education available to every primary school age child in Uganda. We built hundreds and hundreds of school buildings and provided teachers in places where there had never been organized education. The World Bank can tell you where every shilling went."

The Governor asks if we would like a glass of wine with the meal, the one part of his hospitality that makes Ben cringe for the Reverend says true Christians in Uganda avoid all forms of alcoholic beverages. I am seriously tempted but I politely, reluctantly, as a visiting missionary, decline the Governor's offer. "Rev. Ben does not approve of my thirst for the fruit of the vine," the Governor said. "But I must remind him the Bible encourages us to imbibe. Look at First Timothy 5:23: 'Stop drinking only water and use a little wine because of your stomach and your frequent illnesses.' You see, I do this for my health," he says with a wry grin.

He is a gracious host, asking his guests what they think of Uganda. I told him I was surprised to find bright cities teeming with commerce, tens of thousands of people working hard from dawn to dusk, universities overflowing with students and I asked, "Why is there not more foreign investment in this country?"

"Ah," he replied, the grin now gone. "You should ask my friend Dr. Maggie that question."

"Governor," I replied, "I have. The Economic Development Director says after ten years of hard labor, she is making progress. But I still don't understand why companies that scour the world for cheap labor and emerging markets haven't found this place."

Mutebile thought for a minute and then said, "The usual answers are – people set up in South Africa or Kenya to be close to the ports implying that if your country doesn't have a port, it is not worthy of investment. Yet Japan has found us. There are Toyotas everywhere. India has found us – except for a few years, they and the Brits got us going with tea and cotton. The Saudis own much of the real estate in downtown Kampala. Iran is here. Libya is here. Even China has found us. The real answer to your question though is Western business people tend to look at Africa as a whole, lumping all the sub-Saharan countries into one stereotypical view. So the long past sins of Amin mingle with today's religious war in Nigeria, the unbridled AIDS epidemic in Botswana, the genocide in Darfur, the wallowing instability of Congo, the last decade's civil war in Rwanda and the bad track records of governments throughout the continent and they are deterred from looking any closer. You are from Chicago, no? People still know that city for Al Capone, yes?"

I acknowledge, "Touché."

"It has taken us more than two decades," he continued. "But Uganda has reached a point with its financial and communications infrastructure to begin billing itself as the exception to the African stereotype. We were the first to conquer the AIDS epidemic. Our gross domestic product grows at more than 5% a year, 9% in 2007. Inflation is kept in check at 5-6% exclusive of food or fuel. And our people are saving money in banks more than ever before in our history. They are rewarded with up to 14% interest on their accounts. We have 20 active Rotary International Clubs in Kampala alone. Our East African trade alliance which includes Sudan, Kenya, Tanzania and Rwanda is already showing results. We hope to be pumping oil out of the ground from our large Western reserves in a few short years. But what we need is one brand name Western company to see the potential in this place and come set up shop. One bold visionary like the men who tamed the wild American west with their railroads and their stockyards. One gutsy gold rush forty-niner. Just one. That man's success would attract others for sure."

Then he added: "Are you sure you won't join me in a little glass of wine?"

The next day we were awakened by the five a.m. *Muezzin* calling the Muslim faithful to prayer and in the process waking up the roosters and dogs. Soon we are back among the smells of cooking meat, the sounds of traffic and shouting and American rap music, the kaleidoscopic colors of the clothes, the heaps of fresh fruits, the open storefronts, the perpetual motion of tens of thousands of people walking, on bikes, on motorbikes, riding in the backs of trucks, and the glimpses of how people eke out survival by hawking rubber toys or Dockers for $2.50 from the middle of the street.

"Oh, it took me so long to get home," my friend Phinehas remarked. "There was a jam." He meant, of course, a traffic jam. To have him remark on such a condition is noteworthy because the city is one perpetual traffic jam. For this one to be exceptional must have made him consider pitching a tent in the median and starting a fire for tea.

I remember one night, having been in Kampala for a week. We had an appointment to join a new Christian fellowship being held in a neighborhood on the other side of the city. Getting across town meant diving into the morass of humanity and working our way through it. There was no way around. We should have started early to give ourselves time to endure the struggle, but in the African way, there is no time to think ahead, and so we were late. Stuck. At night. Sitting. Surrounded by idling vehicles burning $6.00 per gallon gasoline, being passed by children on foot toddling after their ambling parents. Anchored outside a small grocery store, it felt like we were on a stake-out, watching people come and go. My mind kept wondering, "Which one's the perp?" I wanted a donut.

After an hour of going nowhere but knowing we were expected somewhere, the blatant waste of it all welled up in me. The "this is interesting, I will absorb it all as a traveler who enjoys these things" side of me was overpowered by the "this is stupid – a generation of no urban planning, too many people, no sense of order, nobody in charge, sitting in a car when we could have probably walked there already, the fluorescent-lit shops, the greasy air and the Nigerian sitcoms blaring on unseen televisions, I was clearly agitated. Ben noticed and said, "What is wrong, Mzee?"

"I am so frustrated," I confessed. "This is stupid. We are going nowhere." What I wanted to say is "You backward, over-populating, idiotic people... if you don't care to fix this mess, you deserve to suffer with it. You keep asking for help but you do nothing with it. I quit. Have a nice, poor, disease-ridden, hopeless, futureless life." That speech might have been delivered by any of forty Colonial governments from England, Belgium, Germany, France, Portugal and Holland between

1959 and 1963 when most of the countries in sub-Saharan Africa became independent and were left to manage their own affairs.

Ben said calmly, "Remember, Mzee. We are not organized."

"Aaaay-men, Brother," I replied. The bus erupted in laughter. We hadn't moved an inch. In time, we did reach the Fellowship where over 100 people had also arrived late and filled the time with prayer and song. They fed us. They honored us with gifts. They prayed us away. And I realized I still had a lot to learn.

It has taken awhile, but I have since determined the terms "organization, management, opportunity, business, enterprise and efficiency" as we in the West apply them are differently-shaped concepts to the vast majority of people in Uganda. People from the West become frustrated with the Africans' lack of concern about such things, but it is not that they don't care about them; they just view them and execute them differently, in their own way, a way we are not used to. It is important to note that pre-Colonial Uganda was an orderly society of farmers and herdsmen governed by hereditary kings. Life didn't need to be "organized" because everyone knew what they had to do to contribute to the community. They did as their fathers and mothers had done before them for hundreds of years. The king made all the big decisions and was the all-powerful judge in disputes. The people just lived life from birth to death without any concern for or measure of time.

In 1895, the rhythm of the centuries here abruptly changed when Uganda became a British Protectorate, a kind of junior business partner to Great Britain. This meant that for the next 65 years, the country's economic engine was crafted and run by foreigners who basically told the local people what to do. The people, used to obeying the king, complied.

The growing of cash crops for export or processing, the erecting buildings with multiple floors, the building of railroads was all new to this bucolic society. Yes, there were universities and yes, there was a growing professional expertise in Ugandan society, but when the Brits left after independence, they took any innate sense of Western entrepreneurship or organization with them. It was as if the carnival came to town and let the locals hand tools to the engineers who ran the rides and then the engineers went home to leave the workers to run the rides they had not cared to build in the first place. Thus, Uganda's world-trade-based economy faltered. Greedy potentates and idiot dictators, many of whom were transition people - European-educated and tribal-cultured, reaped the rewards of whatever resources there were, ruled ineptly for the next 20 years and ensured that a bad situation got worse.

The onset of AIDS wiped out an entire generation of competent people and caused further setbacks. So while the industrialized West and Asia have bolted together a global economy over the last four decades, this part of the world was left behind. I began to realize that if I am frustrated having been exposed to it for a week, how frustrated must the people be who must live with it every day. They cope but they do not like it. And as a people, they are working hard to catch up.

Now, into this evolving culture come the *Mzungus*. That's my tribe, the white-skinned people. On the national level we come as advisors, consultants, aid workers and emissaries. We bring money and the promise of hope, but as you'll read later on, we also come with our agendas, our strategies, our version of expertise and, quite frankly, an institutional paternal arrogance which, more often than not, clashes with the local culture.

A few of us come to Uganda called "The Pearl of Africa" by Winston Churchill as tourists, mostly from Europe, adventure travelers interested in staying in exotic hotels, seeing water falls, rafting the Nile River, climbing the Rwenzori Mountains, camping the national parks, spying on gorillas or shopping the crafts market. Tourists tend to keep to themselves and stay within the boundaries of their tour package. While tourism is good for the local economy, these visitors rarely get to experience the real treasure of the country which is its people.

Many more of us come as mini-missionaries with the express purpose of meeting local humanitarian needs. It is amazing to me to realize that thousands of people will annually spend thousands of dollars to fly across oceans and continents with boxes of medicine or clothing or tools or books in order that they can demonstrate to people they have never met what "love thy neighbor" means, even if it is just for a few weeks. We go to build schools, libraries, churches, orphan homes, to dig wells, teach, preach or just hold babies. Some *Mzungus* emigrate here to work as missionaries for the rest of their lives.

In addition, there are hundreds of faith-based non-government organizations (NGOs) here, some of them quite large, dedicated to helping people live spiritually and physically healthier lives. Global organizations such as World Vision, Compassion International, the Navigators or Life International (Campus Crusade) may be based in the *Mzungu* West but they operate here with Ugandan management and staff. There are also hundreds of home-grown NGOs such as TASO (The AIDS Services Organization) and UWESO, (Uganda Women's Effort to Save Orphans) that employ thousands of people. Taken altogether, humanitarian work is big business in Uganda. More importantly, the nation's leadership acknowledges that without such outside aid, millions of Ugandans now alive would have died from disease or poverty long ago.

For visitors to Uganda, it doesn't take very many days before one becomes changed by The Africa Effect. I'm not sure if it's the noisy bustle of the cities, waking up to the sounds of life – roosters, birds, dogs, the *Muezzin*, mothers calling across a courtyard, babies crying, the incessant energy spent on earning a meager living, the dazzling white smiles accompanied by limitless hospitality or the binary simplicity of the place: work or die, eat or starve, pray with hope or wither away, but this place changes those of us who visit from the West.

Sometimes the change comes hard.

After a week of moving bricks and digging trenches, working shoulder to shoulder with local people of a very remote village, Rhonda was touched deeply by the many children wandering around the village in torn and ragged cast-off clothing. She and her teen-aged daughter had brought clothing collected from churches the US to give to children and had already handed over most of it to the program directors for distribution as they saw fit.

When it came time to depart, Rhonda and her daughter were seated in the van along with eight other people and a mountain of luggage. Ben came by to say farewell. Along the way, he noticed Rhonda had a stack of used clothing in her lap. "Why do you have clothing in your lap?" he asked. Rhonda replied, "We're going to toss T-shirts to needy children as we go down the road."

"Rhonda," he said softly. "You have a big heart. You have done great work here this week. But I must ask you to please do not do that."

"But," she said insistently, "We have clothing left."

"Yes," Ben replied. "And the people here will be glad to have it, but not in this way."

"Well, we're going to do it anyway," she huffed. A van load of people cooking in the equatorial sun silently witnessed the exchange.

"Look," Ben said, leaning in the door. "If you do this, you will set a bad precedent for both the people in this village and also for every missionary team that comes after you. If you want to give someone a gift, give it gladly. Personally. Not tossed out the window of a van."

"Well..." Rhonda began to rebut.

"No," the Reverend said, not quietly. "I *beseech* you. Do not do this thing. Find a school or a church where you can drop these things and let the people in charge distribute to the neediest. Let it be a gift. Please. Okay?" Tears were rolling down Rhonda's cheeks. Her daughter sniffled, with hands fingering the shirts in her lap. Rhonda closed her eyes and nodded in reluctant agreement. "Okay," Ben said, adding: "Dear heavenly father," he prayed spontaneously, "We know you love people with big hearts. Please be with this team as they travel on this journey to Kabale Town. Be with them, comfort them, and give them an opportunity to do everything they want to accomplish while they are in Uganda. We pray this in Jesus' name." Most of the sweating people mumbled a quiet "Amen."

"*Tugyende*," I said. "Let's go." The sliding door to the van slammed shut and the people were glad to be moving.

It was a bright, dry day. Green valleys ripe with pineapple and sorghum and potatoes stretched off between the mountains. The van sped past children alongside the road who waved and smiled, many yelling "*Mzungu!*" when they saw us. These children would have been the ones to see T-shirts flying out of the windows. Light chatter could be heard inside the van but silent tears continued to stream from Rhonda's eyes.

Some 20 minutes into the journey, Dennis the driver pointed out an enormous dust cloud coming toward us. It was a large Mercedes semi truck and tandem trailer barreling down the gravel road, raising a cloud of dust so thick that, when it passed us, we needed to slow nearly to a crawl until the way became visible again. Coming to the rise of the next hill, the van started to choke and sputter. "Mzee, I believe we have dust in the filters," Dennis said. We were more than 25 kilometers from the nearest town, 25 kilometers from the nearest service station. The van jerked. The engine coughed. One passenger voiced the fears of all, "What if we don't make it to town?"

"I will have to check it," Dennis said. The van moved alright at a very slow speed, but the moment Dennis pressed hard on the gas pedal, the engine hesitated and gasped. We limped along over the top of a small rise and then, coasting downhill, Dennis turned into a driveway. A primary school. With kids at recess playing. We exited the van because Dennis needed to lift the seats for access to the engine. Monica, one of the program staff returning home to Mbarara with us from Kishanje, quietly asked one of the older children to fetch the headmaster.

Within a quarter hour, a youngish man in a purple shirt and black necktie introduced himself in well-formed British English as Victor, the headmaster of this school. As is the custom, we introduced ourselves to him and to the group of a hundred children in pink uniforms, each of us stating our name and that we were visitors from America. Monica whispered something to Rhonda and her daughter, a nod, then to Victor, another nod. Within minutes, a black duffel, filled to bursting, appeared from the van. Rhonda and her daughter and Victor carried it into the school office, returning a few minutes later with an empty duffel.

Dennis started the van and gunned the engine. There were no hiccups.

The children sang a greeting song. We took photos and said farewell. In minutes we were back on the dusty road to Kabale Town traveling at flank speed. Cheerful chatter filled the van.

From my co-pilot seat I turned around and said to the saints, "Does everyone realize what just happened?" No one spoke. "Really, does anyone get it?" Still no one spoke. "Does anyone have goose bumps on their arms like I do?" No words.

"People, we have just witnessed God at work," I said. "He responded to the generous hearts of Rhonda and her daughter. He answered Ben's prayer. He provided for the children of this school. He gave Victor a way to inspire his students with the generosity of strangers and brighten the day for a dozen orphan kids. He answered all those prayers in about 30 minutes from the time they were spoken. Rhonda, dry your tears. You and your daughter caused a miracle. Amen?" The vanload shouted, "AMEN."

I was in that van for seven more days and the engine never faltered.

When we return home, we are startled at how clean the airport is. The roads are remarkably smooth. There are operating traffic lights and drivers obey them. There are no iron grates on the windows. The meat is tender. There is plenty of water and electricity. Toilets flush and showers are hot. No one tries to sell you bananas or roasted meat-on-a-stick at the stop sign. And then you hear the overweight children begging their overweight mothers for candy. You hear them bicker because one has more M&Ms on his ice cream cone. You notice few people are walking and when they do, they pass each other on the sidewalk like ghosts. One half hour of television news filtered through our new Ugandan point of view makes it look like Americans are a nation of bored, overfed sports worshipers whose leaders can be as self-centered, arrogant and corrupt as any in the third world.

We miss the welcomes, the thick tropical air full of smells, the warm greetings, the laughter, the singing, the spontaneous prayer, and the exercise of walking from place to place, sometimes with the surprise of a small child who puts her hand in yours and wants to walk along. We want to tell people how we feel, but realize they cannot understand. We aren't home for very long before we long to go back.

# A Christian Country

*"Send missionaries, many missionaries,*
*to bring Africa into the light."*
- Henry Morton Stanley, 1875

I thought I lived in a Christian country, one nation under God, but I had met Ben and he was unlike any American Christian I had ever known. He said simply, "Come home. Meet God there."

Indeed, God is everywhere in Uganda. The stores are named God's Mercy Unisex Salon, Free Way Pool Joint. There is the New Life Bar. Vehicles have "Born Again" or "Jesus Cares" stenciled boldly on the windshield. A sign on the door of a print shop states, "The Blood of Jesus Covers This Business." People greet each other with "praise God" in English or any of 40 tribal dialects. Popular music pouring from loudspeakers in the markets is mostly American or locally-produced Christian praise music. Every meal taken in private is prayed over and more often than not, meals in public as well. You see people seemingly talking to themselves but when you get closer, you hear their words and they are in dialog with God.

For me, such outward expression of gratitude to God was freeing. Here I did not feel apologetic or awkward in giving

thanks for a meal at the luncheon buffet joint. Here, it bright-
ened my day to greet someone with *Mukama asiimwe* (Praise
God) just for the privilege of receiving *Asiimwe munonga*
(Praise Him indeed) in return. And here I was challenged to
think about how God has worked in my life because the people
here – young people in schools and adults in their homes –
really want to know such things about each other.

It is common for occasional evangelists – whether it is
local Scripture Union workers or American visitors – to be
invited into schools to speak to students about life, the Bible
and Biblical things, to pray and sing with them. This is so
different from the comfortable suburban place I live where
school administrators are afraid to utter the word "Christmas" on school property. "Here," Ben says, "The headmasters
welcome it. We are a nation of faith and where exposing our
young people to the stories and faith lessons of others, especially visitors from another part of the world, is a vital part of
our children's education."

I can attest that the value of visitors but are we really evan-
gelizing? We have no Jehovah's Witnesses tracts and we do
not travel in pairs like black-suited Mormons. It seems all
too natural, but it is okay, like the difference between push
marketing of God's word and pull marketing of people hungry
to hear how God is working in the lives of others. Here, it is
almost as if Jesus is a serial superhero and people cannot wait
to hear next week's episode of how he has transformed the life
of another person – even from across the world. Live testimony. Real witness. Can this be evangelism?

It certainly can. And it is easy here because no matter
what someone is doing – building, digging, teaching, traveling, the subject of Jesus arises and, almost more than the

words that are said, the behavior of the people involved makes the message. For example, I met a group of teenagers on a mission trip from their church that arrived loud and laughy with slouches and sneers, making inane jokes amongst themselves. They traveled well enough because their senses were engaged. But when there was downtime, they looked at each other for entertainment – cards or sharing music on iPods. They labored well during the day trying to be useful, but they always seemed distracted. A few girls played with some local children for awhile, but for the most part, they were aloof. Upon their return, when asked how the experience was for them, most answered, "It was okay." The local people cannot remember the names of any of these visitors.

Contrast that with a group of young people just out of college who came the following year with no other agenda than "to be with the people." They too helped build walls. They too helped move the earth. But they devised games with children. They helped with homework. They taught simple lessons. They participated in Bible studies. And they returned home bathed in Christian spirit. Years have passed and still the local children ask after these people.

I was asked to preach one Sunday at All Saints Cathedral in Kampala. I am not a trained sermonizer or minister or cleric and, even as an ordained elder in the Presbyterian Church, I have no formal Biblical education beyond adult Sunday school. But having been invited, I thought it would be worth the try.

When compared with cathedrals on other continents, this building did not fit the stereotype. There was not one flying buttress. No gargoyles. No six-story sanctuary, apse, nave or chapel. No sixteenth century roseate windows, no bell tower, crypts, frescoes or gold-leaf altar hand-carved by three generations of tradesmen.

It was a white stucco building with a red tile roof on the top of a hill. Inside, it looked like an English country church where timbers arched two stories high. Bed sheets hanging from the trusses displayed a hymn's words from an opaque projector.

Behind the church is the state house complex where the President and his staff manage the affairs of the nation. During the Idi Amin era, the few parishioners who came to church on Sunday could hear the cries of people being tortured in the government buildings and the torturers with the hammers could hear the hymns of the faithful through the dungeon windows. Today, the music of a thousand voices washes over the hill four times every Sunday morning while the guards at the gates often sing along.

Also behind the church, behind a chain-link fence, were giant eucalyptus trees fifty feet tall where African gray parrots squawked in their nests. The state house grounds were manicured and green, a verdant no-man's land, open space between the fence and the President's compound. The guards watching there may have been singing on Sunday, but they also carried automatic rifles with banana clips.

This is the church where Ben married his wife Lilian.

We arrived early and parked in one of the few spaces next to the church. By the time we were ready to leave, cars were parked three deep. Exiting the compound meant going through a gate which someone had blocked with his parked car. When at last the car was moved, the gate opened, another tried to take the space but was shooed away. We watched in wonder as people tried to drive two ways on the one-lane access road. "Why doesn't someone organize this traffic to be two-way with designated parking?" I asked. Ben smiled and shrugged his shoulders. The message was clear: relax, this is the way it is.

The Senior Pastor, Rev. Canon Alfred Kweteisa greeted me warmly and gave me a gold-colored preaching robe to wear. The zipper was broken. My name was in the bulletin. I was escorted to one of the hard-backed wooden chairs whose design I was sure hadn't changed since the apostles sat there. A choir in purple robes made angelic music accompanied only by a goatskin drum.

When it was time for Rev. Kweteisa to introduce me, he told the congregation my name was "Murder." He realized that didn't come out quite right, so he tried again. But his Luganda got in the way. I didn't realize it at the time, but the Bantu dialects have a hard time with "Ls and Rs." L comes out R so Mr. Mutebile is Mr. Moota-beeri. The Ankore district has been pronounced Ankole for so long, it is now spelled that way on signs. Kare is pronounced "Colley." A preacher referred to Jesus as "The King of Groly." I saw a bus for Holiday Tours named "Holiday" on the front and "Horiday" on the side. That was why the Rev. Canon introduced me as Murder. I took the steps to the pulpit with a kind glance and smile at my introducer, hoping people had read the bulletin and understood I was not actually a deadly sin.

I stood there that day and thanked God for sending a Ugandan man to America to touch the hearts of people who wanted to come and see the reality of this piece of Africa for themselves and thereby become touched by the spirit of a people. I told the congregation we had to come to see if there were any more like him around (to polite chuckles).

I tried to convey a message of hope that the people assembled might see themselves as part of a much larger congregation of believers in Christ around the world who sing the same songs, say the same prayers and believe they will end up in the same place – as those assembled here. It was meant to be inspirational and worldly. People were courteous at the end but I had the feeling they missed hearing an emotionally-delivered Biblical message from one of their countrymen. The greater lesson for me was evangelistic: if I can stand up before 2,000 people and tell my story, then anyone can.

People here pray for safe travel, for each other, for kids in school, for their work, for the weather, for "general mercies." They thank God for giving them each day. They thank Him in advance for things they would like to have happen. "Dear Lord, we ask that the tired brakes on this vehicle last through the weekend. Thank you for watching over us." A church service often includes a thanksgiving offering where a family tangibly thanks God for the arrival of a child, the curing of a disease, the return of family from overseas.

Worship here is joyous. The music is lively. People dance. People jump. I've been to Gospel Churches in the U.S. where people raise their arms and sing their hearts out but before I went to Uganda, I had seen just one person jump for God, Ben the Ugandan.

In the countryside, the kids hum tunes like *Webare Jesu* (Thank you Jesus). I came upon a man, a carpenter, busy running a crew of people putting in the structure for a ceiling in a large building. The tools were crude: a hammer and a saw. The men worked on the construction site in bare feet. The sawhorses, the lifting devices, the scaffold and the ladders were lashed-together tree branches. Yet he was so overcome by the work his crew was doing, he burst into dance while singing *Webare Jesu*.

There is another song that people sing in acknowledgement of any good thing. It is an expanded way, the Ugandan way, of saying "That's cool, or Hallelujah." It goes like this:

*Tukutendereza. Jesu.*
*Jesu orimwana, gwandiga*
*Omusai gugwai guniza,*
*Nebaza, Omolokozi.*

It means: "We thank God for everything in the blood of Jesus. This was the song Rev. Ben and his friend Denis were singing at the airport on our arrival ...*omolokozi.*

For Westerners, it is a gnawingly curious thing to meet, watch and live with people who need faith in their lives just as much as they need air and food and water. We hear about "practicing your faith" but to see it – and then become a part of it – changes one's innate understanding of faith. One wizened missionary girl said, "I never saw the face of God until I got here."

In attempting to describe faith, CS Lewis wrote, "I think all Christians would agree with me if I said that though Christianity seems at first to be all about morality, all about duties and rules and guilt and virtue, yet it leads out of all that into something beyond." But here's the clincher: "One has a glimpse of a country where they do not talk of those things, except perhaps as a joke. Every one there is filled full with what we should call goodness as a mirror is filled with light. But they do not call it goodness. They do not call it anything. They are not thinking of it. They are too busy looking at the source from which it comes."[3]

Faith here does not treat God like Santa Claus: "God, give me stuff. God, help me make this putt." Instead, it is a faith of gratitude: "Thank you for this day. Thank you for the rain. Thank you for the food on this table. Thank you for these shoes, this school, these grades, these friends." Often it is thanks in advance. "Thank you for bringing fish into my nets today. Thank you, Lord, for protecting me as I go out into the world."

Still, people here do not hesitate to ask for the things they need. The Bible says, "Ask and it shall be given to you," so people ask, slipping into prayer during the course of a conversation: "Lord, we need this meeting to go well. Lord, bring people alongside us that we may magnify the work we are doing in your name. Lord, we are working hard to feed our family. Please make my crops abundant. Lord, give us good traffic through Kampala today so we may be on our way." And you know what? Even more bizarre than watching people live their lives with prayer on their lips, is the fact that very more often than not – the prayer is granted. Diseases are cured. Crops are abundant. Orphans find homes. Fish fill the nets. Money shows up to pay for essentials. The brakes last through the weekend. And even if the prayer is not granted as asked, God is still good.

If you question people in Uganda about their faith, they will look at you quizzically like, "what, God doesn't answer your prayers?" People here expect God to come through because he always does. In their mind, they are talking to a

3   C.S. Lewis, *Mere Christianity*, Harper Collins Edition 2001, pages 149-150. Original copyright 1952 C.S. Lewis Pte.Ltd.

divine, all-powerful parent who cares about them, who listens to them, who makes a judgment on all requests – yes, no, or maybe in time – every time. He is dependable. He is essential. God delivers. There is a direct connection between the prayers and the result. Every day.

As I watch a people organically living their lives in faith, I cannot help but recall that, in answer to the question, "Why don't we feel God in our lives in America?" the Christian author Philip Yancy wrote, "God apparently goes where he's wanted."

People will tell you matter-of-factly the Bible says God takes care of the flowers and he provides a nest for the sparrow... are we not as precious to Him? He takes care of the children here – even those in the most dire conditions – God takes care of the child-headed families living in a rude hut and those scratching for food. In our eyes, God has abandoned these people, but in their minds, there is no doubt God is present and hard at work taking care of his faithful family.

Various publications have recently acknowledged the faith-based culture in Uganda, one stating that "religious fervor "has appeared and is growing recently..." but the authors are wrong. Christ was introduced here more than 100 years ago and became indelibly etched into the culture more than eight decades ago.

In 1875, at the beginning of his famous trek across Africa, Henry Morton Stanley, the journalist who is famous for uttering "Dr. Livingstone, I presume," was the first white explorer to circumnavigate Lake Victoria. At the north end of the lake where he followed the footsteps of another British explorer, James Speke, the discoverer of Lake Victoria as the source of the Nile River, Stanley came upon the Kingdom of Buganda whose king, or *Kabaka*, was named Mtesa. The King had been first visited by Speke some ten years earlier and so was not unfamiliar with the sight of white-faced British explorers. This is perhaps the reason Stanley's party was greeted formally by 1,000 armed men in war canoes. In Stanley's words, Mtesa was "a generous prince and a frank and intelligent man, who was tall and somewhat nervous, dressed in a black robe with a gold belt."[4] Mtesa claimed to be a follower of Islam, yet in the course of their conversations over a period of weeks, the subject of religion was discussed at length, whereupon Stanley set about persuading Mtesa that Christianity was much superior to Islam. The message was received openly by the King which prompted Stanley to write a letter to his editors in London called "a stirring call for missionaries to be sent to Uganda." The letter is a revealing insight into Stanley's view of what Africa needed to "bring it into the light" as he called not just for people willing to convey the word of God but also people with skills and a sense of enterprise. This single act was the first step toward colonialization of the region.

We get the impression King Mutesa was less interested in religion than in perpetuating and protecting his kingdom since, before Stanley arrived, when most of his visitors were Arab slavers and traders, it benefited him to be Islamic. When it seemed the British were coming and they could both bring trade and keep the Egyptians from encroaching on the north, it benefited him to be Christian.

After describing how Mtesa was earlier converted to Islam, Stanley claimed that he had defeated the Arab influence by a single interview with the king. The Ten Commandments was written on a board at Mtesa's request so that he could

---

4    *Stanley, An Adventurer Explored*, Richard Hall (1975, Houghton-Mifflin) p. 40

study them daily, together with the Lord's Prayer and Christ's injunction – 'thou shalt love thy neighbor as thyself.' A few years later Mtesa was to show where his real faith lay by having hundreds of people sacrificed in the belief that this would save him from serious illness.[5]"

Stanley's letter was one of the most significant messages to come out of Central Africa in the second half of the nineteenth century. More than £25,000 – a huge sum for the day - was quickly raised in Britain to speed the Gospel to Mtesa's subjects. In the years to come, missionaries would be murdered and converts put to death, but the blood of the martyrs proved to be the seeds of the church and the numbers of believers grew rapidly beyond the borders of their own kingdom in a movement called the East Africa Revival.

The complete story of the East Africa Revival is told well and in great detail in *A Gentle Wind of God: The Influence of the East Africa Revival* by Richard K. McMaster, but I need to include the highlights here to give a sense of the deeply ingrained sense of Christian conscience that lies in the hearts of the Ugandan people even until today.

In 1893, the Buganda Christians sent 260 evangelists at their own expense to 85 preaching stations, rapidly becoming the native "Church of Uganda." The first African deacons were ordained in that year and the first priests in 1896. By 1909, the Native Anglican Church of Uganda had over 100,000 adherents. Not only was the entire Bible translated and circulated by tens of thousands, but there was also extensive religious literature. The Church of Uganda was governed by its own synod which was the only constitutional body in Uganda that successfully cut across tribal boundaries. European

---

5    Ibid, p. 42

missionaries participated on equal terms with the African converts in the governing of the church.

McMaster continues: "Unlike other African countries where the gospel was slow to take root, the Protestant church in Uganda was unique in the speed, scale and sheer enthusiasm of its early missionary movement and in the production of an ordained clergy by 1900. They provided many of the personnel for the expansion of Christian missions in Kenya, Tanganyika and Ruanda-Urundi.

"By the late 1920s, Christians were still only a third of the people of Uganda but they had a disproportionate share of social, economic and political power and dominated the government. All the members of the Buganda governing council and nearly all the chiefs were Christians. The Church of Uganda was comparatively rich and this prosperity brought problems with native missionaries as one Anglican hospital director said, "being pulled away by growing wealth, racial feelings and bad habits."[6]

This was the mood of the church and the Christian community in Uganda when, in September, 1929, three people from separate walks of life came together to ignite a spark that would become the East Africa Revival also known in Uganda as the *Balokole* Revival *Balokole* is a Luganda word meaning "The Saved People."[7]

Joe Church was a young British medical doctor with a closely-cropped mustache, the product of the best of English education and culture, but instead of settling into a medical

6    McMaster, Richard K. *A Gentle Wind of God: The Influence of the East Africa Revival,* Herald Press, Scottsdale, PA 2006 p. 31

7    Ward, Kevin, **"Obedient Rebels: The Relationship between the Early "Balokole" and the Church of Uganda: The Mukono Crisis of 1941"** *Journal of Religion in Africa,* Vol. 19, Fasc. 3 (Oct., 1989), pp. 194-227 http://links.jstor.org/sici?sici=0022-4200(198910)19%3A3%3C194%3A%22RTRBT%3E2.0.CO%3B2-F

career in England, he dedicated his life to the Lord as a missionary doctor at Gahini Hospital in Northeastern Rwanda. In early 1928, the rains failed and, by the time the dry season began, famine gripped the region. By November, a thousand hungry refugees paused every day at Gahini Hospital on their way to Uganda. "They crawl to us from miles round and by the time they arrive, they have scarcely sufficient strength in their shrunken, shriveled bodies to hold out their hands," Church reported. The missionary and his wife worked with church leaders to set up a famine relief appeal. By 1929, the famine was over and he went to Kampala for a few days of rest.

Mabel Ensor was an Irish-born Church Missionary Society teacher and evangelist who taught a regular Bible study at the Anglican Church in Kampala on Namirembe Hill. She had come to Uganda as a nurse working in the nearby Mengo Hospital. In her classes, she spoke of the church as "backslidden," with baptized Christians returning to polygamy, witchcraft and false worship and inspired her student to pray for renewal and revival. Joe Church attended the class whenever he was in Kampala and often spoke on the topic of surrendering all and coming out for Jesus. One of Miss Ensor's students was a well-to-do government official named Simeoni Nsibambi.

As the son of a Christian chief and a large landowner, Nsibambi was a rich young man who dressed in the latest British styles for gentlemen. Like Joe Church, Nsibambi was the product of a culture that honored education and civility. He lived with his wife, Eva and their children in a large house on Namirembe Hill near the Anglican Cathedral. Simeoni and Eva devoted themselves to the work of the Good Samaritan Society in Kampala, sang in the cathedral choir and led Bible Studies. Raised in a Christian home and educated in

Missionary schools, Nsibambi had several points of inspiration in his life, but he pointed to October 3, 1927 when he wrote, "As from today, I desire to be genuinely holy and never intentionally do anything unguided by Jesus." This thought was still in his head when he heard Joe Church speak to Mabel Ensor's Bible class.

Later, when the drought was over, a discouraged and exhausted Joe Church returned to Kampala for respite and rest and, once again spoke at Miss Ensor's Bible Class. In a letter to a friend in England, he wrote: "Yesterday a rich *muganda* in government service rushed up to me at Namirembe and said he had heard me speaking at a small meeting run by Miss Ensor. I had spoken about surrendering all and coming out for Jesus. He said he had done so and had great joy in the Lord and had wanted to see me ever since. And then he said in his own words that he knew something was missing in the church and in himself; what was it? Then I had the great joy of telling him about the filling of the Spirit and the Victorious Life."[8]

Before he left Kampala to return to Gahini, Joe Church met a missionary who asked him: "What have you done to Nsibambi? He's gone mad and is going round everywhere asking people if they are saved. He's just left my gardener." The missionary was not pleased. It was her opinion that Africans were not ready for this teaching about sanctification and the Holy Spirit.

But Nsibambi was earnest about beginning a new life. He gave up wearing shoes to go barefoot like the poor. The *kanzu*, a long white robe replaced his British-tailored suits. He sold many of his possessions and gave away the proceeds. He quit his post in the health department and began a life of daily personal witness in the streets, shops and hospitals of Kampala.

8    McMaster, p. 28

"I feared for the future," Nsibambi said in 1929, "but I finally obeyed. People thought I was crazy but I didn't mind."

In a short time, Nsibambi gathered weekly with thirty or forty Christians to talk about "revival," meaning a renewed life in Christ sometime after accepting Jesus as Lord and Savior. With a philosophy based largely on the book *Lectures on Revival* by Charles G. Finney published in 1835, people went into the streets asking people if they were "living a Victorious life in Christ." Even today, Ugandans speak of being Christians for many years before they were saved. One man quipped, "I've been a Christian for so long, it's time I got saved."[9]

Interestingly enough, even though Nsibambi stimulated the call to revival, he is rarely called its founder. People caught the message without emulating the messenger. Few others gave away their shoes or sold their possessions or donned the *kanzu*. And soon the message reached Gahini where Joe Church and a team of African leaders, one of which was Blasio Kigozi, Nsibambi's younger brother who injected "a new spirit into the hospital staff. One by one they came out for God. Those young Christians were characterized by the same zeal as that first seen in Simeoni Nsibambi." Encouraged by the local Bishop, Joe Church and Nsibambi led retreats and meetings with students in and around Kampala and soon the revival took on a tangible character. In the coming together of two and three or four seeking to know and do God's will, hidden sins confessed led to restitution made for thefts or injuries.[10]

From 1932 to 1936, the revival spread spontaneously through team visits, house groups and large conventions and, with it, grew a wave of public confession that stripped away

9    Ibid, p. 34
10   Ibid, p. 36

all pretense and revealed each person as a sinner in need of the cleansing blood of Jesus. White medical missionaries confessed feeling superior to black hospital staff, they repented this sin and asked forgiveness, creating new relationships that altered the character of the work. Government clerks and laborers confessed to stealing the property of others. Respected church leaders acknowledged sins of lust. Employers admitted cheating those who worked for them.[11]

The revival spread to hospitals, schools, markets and homes. One of the most memorable gatherings took place over the span of a week in September, 1935 in Kabale town. Imagine a non-denominational Christian Woodstock. Instead half a million free spirits taking over Yasgur's Farm in upstate New York, a thousand spirit-filled people from Northeast Rwanda and Southwest Uganda overtook the town of Kabale. This time is remembered as the hour a spiritual bomb was dropped to become the epicenter of the Christian quake in the region. A young man named Festo Kivengere was attending Kigezi High School in Kabale at the time and recalls:

"Our attention was riveted by the shining faces of these men who obviously had spiritual freedom, were in love with God and at peace with one another. We listened wide-eyed at what they had to say. Within a month, people began to weep unexpectedly, dream dreams of Heaven or cry out under conviction until they came to know Christ personally." Students began gathering for prayer and at all hours. They formed teams that went out in all directions speaking of repentance and revival. There were reports of whole congregations praying, trembling, crying out all night. Wherever they went, people were transformed into seeking ways to make restitution for sinful behavior or hurtful decisions. Men approached businesses to

---

11    Ibid, p. 41

return goods or make amends for things that had been stolen years before. Husbands and wives confessed infidelity to each other and begged forgiveness. So many people confessed sins, the countryside was awash in acts of pride that withered and died in the equatorial sun. Families were healed. Individuals were inspired. Hope was revived. Churches swelled with new adherents. And at the center of it all was Jesus.

Interestingly enough, it was in the boarding schools and hospitals that manifestations of revival presented the most difficulties. Missionary teachers and hospital sisters found their entire institutions disrupted while singing and praying went on all night. They sometimes complained about this emotionalism to church authorities. But no missionary could deny that, after the emotion passed, revival left a love and zeal that glowed and burned and left a testimony on the hearts of the people.[12]

Over the years, the East Africa Revival grew organically throughout the region through, as they say, ordinary people obeying God. There were no superstars, no iconic leaders and there was no headquarters for the movement. It was not a sect or a rebellious offshoot of existing Christian thought, but grew within the structure of the Church of Uganda. The Church generally encouraged the idea of revival, but in the 1940s, a major schism between revivalists and the church after 26 *balokole* students training for the ministry at Bishop Tucker Memorial College in Mukono were expelled for being *bajeemu* – rebels. Nevertheless, by the 1950s, revival had become an integral part of the life of the Church of Uganda. Festo Kivengere ultimately became an Anglican Bishop. Bishop Tucker College became Uganda Christian University where, in 2007, Uganda's Prime Minister Apolo Nsibambi, the son of Simeoni and

12   Ibid, p. 44

Eva, spoke during the opening of a new residence hall named after his parents. [13]

The East Africa Revival ripples every year in Mbarara town. I happened to be there the second week of November when the local Anglicans at All Saints Church stage "Evangelism Week." For seven days, this busy, prosperous town of 100,000 people was saturated with the love of Jesus. Fellowships and Bible Studies filled the days. Emulating Nsibambi and Kigozi and Church and countless young people over the years, teams of two or three fanned out through the town, visiting every business and storefront, talking to the *boda boda* drivers at every taxi stand, preaching to every class in every school, and handing out Bibles. An outdoor mini-crusade was held near the center of town, the "skid row" of this place where drunks yelled back at the evangelists and four-foot-tall Maribou storks picked through the garbage. There was an altar call. Two truck drivers come forward. A ranting woman collapsed in convulsions in front of the preacher who immediately changed his message to exhort the demons from her body. At the end of three hours, everyone left, exhausted. Yet the next day was the Evangelism Parade a block long with cars and flatbed trucks full of people singing, dancing and waving palms in the name of Jesus. People joined the parade until it was nearly a half mile long. The same faces of disbelief stared back at us from the curbsides in Uganda as would have stared from any curbside in America. At the end, people strew across a hill to hear sermons delivered from the back of a truck.

---

13   Speech by Apolo Nsibambi September 3, 2007 http://www.newvision. co.ug/D/8/459/584765/East%20Africa%20Revival

Seventy years after the first "spiritual bomb" was dropped, Kabale town once again came alive with the fervor of the East Africa Revival to celebrate the anniversary of the event. Where the first meetings were a celebration of the transforming power of the spirit, the 21$^{st}$ century gathering encompassed much of the month of August with 20,000 people gathering to cry with amazed gratitude that the spirit was alive and stronger than ever despite the rigors of independence, dictators, rebellion, warfare, refugees and the ravages of AIDS. As previously mentioned, the Luganda song *Tukutendereza Jesu,* the rallying hymn for the *Balokole* with its message of "We praise you Jesus" is still sung in Anglican churches and fellowships throughout Uganda. Can there be any doubt why people call Uganda a Christian nation?

This American was, at first, astounded by the overkill. How many times do you need to deliver the same message? I was uncomfortable watching the local preachers walk into shops where people were dealing with customers and asking everyone if they knew Jesus. I grew impatient with the crusade at the dump and was distracted with the garbage-picking storks that looked like pterodactyls as they flew down Main Street.

Then it hit me. The sheer volume of "message," the unwavering joy with which it was delivered, the vast participation, the deliberate effort to present Jesus to every shadow and bowery of town – delivering the message – telling the stories – thanking God on every corner – celebrating His love and His gift, people cannot help but be touched in some way. This conclusion comes from someone who quickly dismisses the Jehovah's Witness when she rings the door bell, who was raised to understand church stops at the sidewalk around the property, who lives in a place where "separation of church and state" means you can't say the word "Jesus" in school or decorate a Christmas tree on government property. Yet here it is: Jesus' name echoing off every building, resounding in every classroom, in your face, take it or leave it, live forever or die. Amen.

I felt woefully inadequate one evening when, sitting around a table after the evening meal, there was no television to cling to yet the evening was young. "Can you sing us a song?" the lady of the house said. The first point of inadequacy came with the request, from people who sing all the time with natural syncopation and harmony that swells the heart and makes one proud. I cannot sing a note. The second problem was, I couldn't think of one appropriate song. They were asking, of course, for a Christian song. I couldn't remember a single Presbyterian hymn from the eighteenth or nineteenth century. I couldn't remember one seven-eleven contemporary praise song. My mind blocked all the Young Life songs. I did think about *Louie Louie* and *Bobby McGee*, but quickly shelved those. After a few pregnant moments of silence, the other *Mzungu* in the room thankfully started *The Green Grass Grew All Around* with all the verses. Somehow the kids just didn't get into the swing of the chorus, "a flea on the dog on the grass that grew all around..." and the evening was saved when our hostess said, "Would anyone like tea?"

Next time I will take a book of praise songs.

# Joyful Evangelism

*"You are Coming to Evangelize the People"*
Rev. Ben Tumuheirwe

I first went to Uganda out of pure curiosity and without any agenda. This is such a different way to travel for someone used to detailed itineraries and timetables, the American mindset always rating the value of service and comparing the experience gained against the price paid for the trip. No, I went on faith. I gave up all control of my time and my expectations, like a traveler on a guided tour with Jesus at the wheel. I got in the van when it was time to go and got out when it stopped and I followed the program somebody had put together. All I knew was what Ben had told me. "You are coming to evangelize the people."

It seemed odd to be going to a Christian country to evangelize people. What could I possibly say to them that they didn't already know? By definition, if they were Christian, they didn't need to hear about Jesus. We've already described Uganda as a Christian country, but many people are Christians by birth or in name only. Similarly to the Christian West, many people consider themselves Christians but do not go to church, study the Bible or openly practice their faith. Most take on the religion of their family, whether Christian, Muslim, Hindu or traditional.

"People, especially young people, need to hear the message of Jesus Christ and how He is working in the lives of real individuals," Ben said. "They need to hear it over and over whether they are committed, working Christians or not. That is what I did for ten years with Scripture Union in schools across the country."

Scripture Union International is an organization that is not well known in the U.S., but operates worldwide with the purpose of bring the Biblical message to school children. Schools here have "SU Clubs" where students have active fellowships, run Bible studies and events. Here, it is okay for evangelists to drop in on a public school with the express purpose of talking about God and Jesus. In fact, the messengers are encouraged to visit as often as they can and if they bring foreign visitors with them, so much the better.

The environment was harmless and friendly enough, but still, for an American, evangelism is not easy. The first opportunity we faced was a small school in Kampala. As visitors, we stood in front of the student body, about 100 children and were formally welcomed with a short song. Ben then asked each of us to introduce ourselves to the assemblage. "Tell them something about your life," he urged. We muttered things about our work, how many children we have, how glad we were to be there. Someone remarked about how in America we have many more things, but we do not have the joy that is present in this room. In time, we began to think about the messages we were conveying... what could be the best message... based on the lives of people from so far away. I could tell everyone was thinking these things because in subsequent schools, churches and fellowships, the revelations became detailed, confessional. They included faith messages of course, but we wove in details of our lives. They became our stories. In a short time, those of us that had a fear of sharing were conveying personal messages to audiences of young people we would never see again and whose faces registered no understanding of what we were saying. How could they, without an American context?

One man told of a problem he had with alcohol and overcame only with the patience of his wife and prayer. A woman told of a problem she experienced with an adopted child, defiant from birth, who needed to be shepherded through periods of drugs and alcohol until the person emerged as a productive adult. One woman launched into a complex monolog of rapidfire Hebrew. What was that? Another normally shy woman fearlessly addressed 1,500 college students with the message: "You are making up your minds what you want to do for your lives right now. As you think, consider these words of God in Philippians 4: I can do everything through Him who gives me strength." A young American man astounded the same audience by speaking to them in their local dialect: *Nkaba ndi omusiisi. Hati, Jesu na kanjuna. Kandi, ningyenda na Jesu.* He had just told them he was a sinner but Jesus saved him and now he walks with Jesus. The looks on the student faces said, 'If he can do it, I can too."

It certainly helps when visitors can speak some of the local language. Uganda is primarily an English-speaking country, that is, British English with African accent, but there are more than three dozen Bantu-based dialects spoken within its borders. We were traveling in the Southwest corner of the country where the most people speak *Rukiga/Runyankole.*

I learned quickly that greeting someone with *Mukama assi-imwe* (Praise the King) would easily elicit a reply of *Asiimwe munonga* (Praise Him indeed) along with a welcome smile and a hand offered in friendship. Greeting groups in this way, then declaring *Ninduga America.* (I come from America) and *Nashemererwa kwija hanu* (I am glad to be here) elicits nods of approval and smiles. Apprehensive children, dour-faced before the camera would light up with smiles when told *Msheka sheka* (smile!). A simple *webare, owesheimwe* (thank you, brother or sister) brings visitors and hosts closer together.

To a body of children whose statistical life expectancy had dropped to less than 40 years, a man testified that he lived the first 47 years of his life in spiritual darkness. A reverend from Chicago shocked his audience when he removed his prosthetic leg and waved it around to show how he had overcome disability. A divorced grandmother told how she had married a man who forced her to join a satanic cult. One woman sang her favorite choir song in a hilltop church on Bwama Island where the sweet, clear sound echoed down the hill and across the still water and women in the fields working their plots of beans and potatoes stopped to listen. American teenagers addressing Ugandan teens in wispy, frightened monotone, being brave, said, "Hi? I'm Tiffany? I'm really glad to see you guys? I just want to say God loves you. That's it."

One man, an inventor more comfortable with pictures than words, sketched his testimony in a mathematical theory with a stub of chalk on a pitted blackboard while students took notes. Another woman, a middle-aged scientist, told how she had seen the pictures of life in Uganda, the beautiful faces of the children and confessed that all the time the person was presenting the pictures she said her heart was beating out of her chest, claiming it was the Holy Spirit telling her to go to Africa.

Speaking last before a room filled with 150 students, a man proclaimed the joy in the room, reminded the young people of the things they had heard from the previous speakers and then he turned serious. He warned students that the warmth they had in being believers in this room would very likely be challenged when they walked outside. He spoke gravely that Satan was watching us all from up there in the rafters, watching and waiting with sparkling eyes a stifled a grin because he knew the words of the believers would not stick. Then he quoted Ephesians 6 about putting on the armor of God – to protect against the evil that would settle over them after the evangelists had gone. A thoughtful silence filled the room.

We Americans evangelized by leading Ugandan kids in their favorite songs and then danced in *Rukiga* fashion with a school headmaster while rhythms from the goat skin drums kept the whole group jumping. A gauntlet of secondary school children in white shirted uniforms welcomed a team of Americans to their celebration even though the visitors were two and a half hours late in arriving. After several hours of fellowship, sharing and prayer on a Wednesday afternoon in Kashasha Village, the entire congregation, hundreds of smiling people, escorted the Americans to their van with song. Of course, in the end, we were the ones being evangelized.

At one primary school, I was followed by a young boy, much taller than his classmates. He made a point of shaking my hand. *Neb'kwetoha*, I asked. What is your name? "My name is Charles," he said softly. Then, "I want to go to America."

"Why?"

"Because you are all rich."

"No," I replied. We have things. You are rich." He shook his head and went to another team member to see if maybe she would take him to America.

At another school, I asked a 12 year-old: "What do you want to do when you finish school?"

"Huh?" he replied, as though he'd never thought about it. It occurred to me he probably hadn't considered his future because everyone he knows becomes a farmer after school. He had no reason to think he could do anything else.

After speaking at a boy's secondary school in Kabale Town, I was surrounded by young men anxious to ask questions. "Mzee, why is everyone in America homosexual?" Somewhat stunned, I replied, "Why does everyone in Africa have AIDS?" It was the young man's turn to be stunned. "We don't," he said. "We aren't," I replied, but then I queried, "Why do you ask?"

"Your church just elected a homosexual Bishop to lead people in their faith." He was referring to the recent appointment of Gene Robinson, a self-avowed homosexual to the position of Bishop overseeing the Episcopal Diocese of New Hampshire. The news had astounded Anglican Church leadership here and resulted in headlines in the largest daily newspaper that read: "Anglican Church of Uganda Severs All Ties with American Episcopal Church." Homosexuality is against the law in Uganda.

"Ah, Bishop Robinson," I replied. "That was for one city. Personally, I'm glad it was not my church or my city and, as far as I know, this is the only homosexual man in such a leadership in our country."

Their next question? "Why does your George Bush want to take over Iraq?"

"I don't believe he does," I replied. "Would your President send Ugandans to join the Americans in fighting there if he did?"

"Is everyone rich in America?"

"No," I replied. "Many of us who visit here need to work a long time to be able to afford the airplane ticket. We are not all movie stars or rock stars. And no, I don't know any."

"You are from Chicago. Do you know Michael Jordan?"

"No, but I have seen him play. Do you know Oprah? She is also from Chicago."

"No. Who is she? But I have a friend, Anne, who lives in America. Do you know her?"

"Can you tell me her last name?"

"No. But she lives in America."

"Do you know where she lives?"

"Yes. In America."

"I'm sorry. I don't know her."

A young man named Daniel pops in: "I like Arra Kelly. And Eminem and Beyonce and Akon and Rhianna and Fifty Cents and Bobby Brown and Ciarra. I want to be a record producer in America."

"You could do that here," I reply.

"Yes, but I would like to do that in America," he said.

Answering these questions and a thousand others, hearing their reality and expressing ours, being able to talk face to face is why we go. We may be people separated by great distances, by different histories, cultures, behaviors and vastly differing living conditions, but it doesn't take long before we realize we are really very much the same. Our values, our desire for family, love, safety and meaning in our lives are universal. We learn that here.

"These messages have power," Ben said. "As you've heard, the people here think everyone in America is rich and comfortable. They don't realize your lives are hard. When you tell them about your reality, and your overcoming problems with faith, it encourages them. It gives them a different picture of America. Life is struggle everywhere. For kids who have been brought up to think all they have to do is to go to America for their lives to be worthwhile, it gives them perspective they would never have any other way. Your willingness to tell your stories makes it okay for students to tell each other their stories."

In 2004, three teams of Americans traveled through Southwest Uganda visiting 44 schools eight churches and a dozen fellowships, offering personal messages of hope and encouragement to more than 50,000 people. On one of those teams, I remember having spent an afternoon in a valley village called Mugyere. There were no roads into this valley, only foot paths which we followed for an hour through banana jungle and rolling hills, the lake sparkling in the distance. Our team spoke to hundreds of children at the primary school and we were enthralled at the secondary school boy's choir, a group that did not exist six months earlier until a local evangelist brought a box full of praise music. We were invited to have food and refreshment at the home of the headmaster and stayed way too long, for the day turned late and dark clouds rolled in between the hills. As we started down the path out of the valley, it started to rain so we ducked under the eaves of nearby building. We waited. It grew darker. Nobody had remembered a flashlight.

One of our party said in a loud, clear voice, "Lord, we have enjoyed doing your work this day, but now we are weary and would like to go home. Please stop the rain and give us a light unto our path in order that we may hike to the van. Thank you, Lord. Amen." We listened to his words, silently adding "Ditto. Amen" and watched the water pour from the eaves. In ten minutes... and I am not making this up... the rain stopped. A last hint of twilight filtered through thinning clouds to light our way across the floor of the valley. As we reached the path leading uphill, the hardest part of the journey, a bright, full moon came out from behind a cloud and lit our way well enough so that even the slowest of us, the clumsiest of us, and those of us with the slipperiest shoes, could find the way. At the top of the path, standing on the road next to the van, Ben simply said, "Thank you Lord. We appreciate your taking care of us." And we all did.

Traveling from place to place, we saw hope in many faces. In many others, however, we saw blank stares. I asked Ben, "How is it possible for these children to hear a message of "Jesus will help you. Turn to Jesus. Have faith in Jesus" when they are sick and hungry and living without parents? How, in fact, can you ponder abstract notions such as an invisible God or making friends with a caring invisible Jesus when your belly is empty?"

"We must feed them and shelter them, of course," he said. "There are always too many but being in need is when faith is born." He reiterated that this is a society where people depend on faith for their lives as much as food, air and water. People these children know can point to situations where God is working. Here come Americans who convey that same message in another part of the world. It brings comfort and obedience. It sows seeds of hope. Nevertheless, he agreed, when hope is not fulfilled, there is discouragement and, for those who have prayed to God time and time again and are seemingly ignored, they can turn away from God.

I hear what he says but I can't help but feel hypocritical. Here come the Americans. We are well-fed, many of us way-too-well-fed, most of us older than the people here can expect to live, having spent more than five million shillings, a fortune to most people here, to come visit, offering words of advice. We, people who have not suffered through famine, sociopathic dictators, dirt-eating poverty, the death of an entire generation of parents, we who are not reminded every day of the struggle of child-headed families, yet we are welcomed, joyously. We stand there in our hundred-dollar sneakers, carrying cameras that cost more than a Ugandan student's annual school fees and speak of our thin spirituality.

When I share these concerns with Ben, he says, "No, Mzee, those things don't matter. If people notice, they forget them quickly when you start to share your life. That is what is important here. The people need to hear how God is working in every person from every nation and they need to hear it every day. This is what inspires young people. This is what helps them to make the right decisions for their lives. It is why we eagerly invited you to come to this place and tell your story in school after school day after day. It is so important."

He reminded me of the times during Missions Week in Mbarara when the Americans walked alongside the Ugandans on a parade through town. Loudspeakers proclaimed the joy of Jesus from the roof of a truck. Cars with 'Jesus is Lord' or 'Jesus is Life' painted on their sides honked their horns. We joked with a cluster of *boda boda* drivers on the corner and prayed with them. We bought oranges from children selling fruit from baskets on their heads and prayed with them. It felt good to spread the joy.

"Spreading joy – it is joyful evangelism that ripples throughout our society," Ben added. "When I ride the bus from Kampala to Mbarara, I wear my priest's collar. These are public buses with people from all walks of life. More often than not, I am asked by someone to pray aloud for the journey and quite often, I am asked to say a few words... make a sermon. I cannot tell you how many times I have preached the miles away. And I cannot tell you how many people have given their lives to Christ before we reach the take-away store in Masaka. Whether I pray or give a talk, people have questions and I am most happy to answer them. We are in a rolling church where people have plenty of time and weighty life issues on their mind. If I were a family counselor, I could set up shop. But I often am able to help people pray their way through their troubles. I cannot tell you how exhausted I am when I finally arrive at my destination. It is a good kind of exhaustion because those are good days for God."

Indeed, recognizing the value of Jesus in our lives – evangelism opportunities – are everywhere here and perhaps this is the greatest lesson we learn when coming from the West. Every moment is an opportunity – a phone call, a visit to a school, a ride on a *boda boda* "Have a blessed day. Oh, you are a Christian? What church do you go to? I don't go to a church. You should try it. There are friends there you have never met yet." Often, these opportunities show up bigger than life.

The second time I went to Uganda, I was late for my departing flight. I had arrived at Entebbe Airport forty-five minutes before departure only to be told the plane was leaving early and I had better hurry or it would leave without me.

The desk clerk rapidly checked my luggage through tagged as "Last Bag." A porter waved me hurriedly through security.

At immigration, the last stop before entering the British Airways passenger lounge, a square-faced man in a starched government shirt studied my passport for what seemed to be an inordinately long time. Come on, I urged in my mind, the plane is about to board. "You are the same age as Khofi Anan's boss," the officer said.

"Excuse me?"

"I said, you are the same age as Khofi Anan's boss... the United Nations."

"Very clever," I replied. "May I have my passport? The plane is boarding."

"Let me ask you," he said, his hand resting on my precious document, clearly unconcerned with my question or the pending departure of my ride home. "Why does George Bush take joy in killing the people of Iraq?" Oh brother, I thought. My plane is leaving and this guy wants to have a deeply philosophical political debate?

"I don't believe he takes joy in watching people die in Iraq, whether they are Iraqis or American soldiers," I said warily. "From what I can tell, our President has used his power to free 25 million slaves and there are a few thousand people who don't like the change. It's a mess right now. But not all Americans are warriors."

"Oh? Why were you in Uganda?"

"To support your Ugandan brothers and sisters in telling the good news of Jesus Christ."

"And were you successful?"

"The people here are being very successful. I only hope we were able to help."

The officer handed over my passport. He stamped my departure card. Then he made a statement, almost a mumbled wish that froze the moment. "I have always wanted to accept Jesus Christ as my Savior," he said.

I was stunned. After two months of talking in churches, on the streets, in the cities, the prisons, the refugee camps, the schools and the universities and receiving so many skeptical looks, here was a soul simply asking to be saved. I set down my bag and relaxed. It was suddenly no longer important if the plane left without me or not. "Would you like to do that right now?"

The square-faced official's face warmed at the thought. "Yes, I would."

"What is your name," I asked.

"Richard."

"Richard, will you pray with me?" He nodded, a slight smile on his lips. "Okay, Richard. Repeat after me..." I enveloped the stranger's hands in my own and bowed my head. Richard did the same. "Dear Heavenly Father, I come before you a sinner." Richard echoed the words. "I have led a life of my own choosing and not to your glory." The echo. "Lord I am empty but I hear you knocking at the door of my heart." Echo. "I invite you in, Lord. I want you to be a part of my life from this moment forward." Echo. "I humbly and intentionally beg you to lead me, guide me, teach me to walk the path of righteousness all the days of my life." Echo. "In the name of the Father, the Son and the Holy Spirit, we pray." Echo. "Amen," we said in unison. I looked up to see tears in the hardened bureaucrat's eyes. But frantic taps from my traveling companions on the glass by the boarding area interrupted the moment; other passengers were already entering the jetway.

"You are a new man today, Richard," I said. "But your journey has just begun. Study God's word. Do you have a Bible?" The man nodded. "Dig it out. Read it. Study it. Also, you need to join a church to be with other believers. Do you live in Kampala?" The man nodded. "Go to All Saints Church on the hill next to the State House. You have friends there you have not met yet. The people will welcome you and nurture you in your faith. In time, they will become your family."

Richard nodded in understanding. We shook hands in the Ugandan way: grip, grip, grip.

"And now I must go. But I will be back in one year. I will want to hear about your life, my brother."

"Go, man of God," the official replied. "And thank you for coming to my country."

As I was whisked through the door to the waiting airplane, a colleague asked me, "What, was that guy giving you a hard time?"

"On the contrary," I said, grinning. "That man and I just gave each other a day neither of us will ever forget."

# When West Meets South

*"Maama Clara, you are welcome."*
Kyarisiima Judith, Kishanje Village

Time oozes in Africa, a concept it we Westerners some are slow to understand. It is our nature to say, "don't just sit there, do something." The African says, "Don't do anything. Sit here and talk to me." It may be this trait, left over from tribal village times when building the relationship, conversing with your neighbor, keeping track of children and relatives, was necessary and made life pleasant. Even today, two men will meet on the street:

*Oreiregye, Sebu* – good morning, sir
*Orriota* – Did you sleep well
*Nderegye* - I slept well.
*Agandi* - How are you
*Nigye* – I am fine
*Oriyo kurungi?* – Are you okay
*Ego ndiyogye* – yes, I am fine
*Murigye mwena* – everybody's good?
*Ego, Turigye* – yes, we are good

*Oriyo nogambakyi* – What's new
*Ndiyo, tinyine shonga yoona* – I don't have any problems.
*Aaaay* – I'm glad
*Aaaay* – I'm glad too
*Kare, Sebu* – Okay, sir.
*Kare kare, mugyendegye* – bye bye, travel safe.

Then they will shake hands the African way – grip, grip, grip.

To Americans, where "Howzit goin?" with a response of "Fine" meets the minimal requirement for common courtesy, the African exchange seems like a repetitive waste of time. To Ugandans, it is courtesy. It is a priority. It is an expression of cultural warmth between acquaintances one can only have in a place where people care more about each other than their busy schedules. Perhaps it is a by-product of people who do not have busy schedules.

Not everyone goes around greeting every other person in this way. As in any other part of the world, there are relatives, friends and acquaintances, co-workers and church members who are naturally glad to see each other. These people are effusive. Then there are good acquaintances who may go through the dialog above. Then there are people you meet for the first time. You shake their hand. If the hands are dirty, they may touch with an elbow. It is like that. The more you get to know them, the more greeting you want to do.

There are children everywhere here. Babies ride in the small of their mothers' backs, tied there with a shawl. As soon as kids can walk, they are put to work. Small chores at first.

Carry this. Hold that. Later it is fetching water or wood or herding goats. Everyone works. The children feel useful and are confident in their abilities.

Children wear whatever they can get for clothing, most of it castoffs from America. Clothing donated to the Salvation Army or Goodwill is bundled in large bales and sent to Africa where it is purchased by clothing brokers and sold at local markets. At first, it is jarring to see a red T-shirt with "Newport Hockey" (the team changed logos), a yellow one with "Inka Kola" (an outgrown souvenir of a trip to Peru) or faded gray with "Syracuse University" (a memory now marred by divorce). The kids have no idea what the writing means; they are glad to have something to wear.

I remarked to the young man advertising Newport: "I like your hockey shirt." He didn't respond. *Mzungus* are always saying things he doesn't understand and it's safest to just not react. "What is your name," I asked.

"Denon," he whispered.

"Do you know hockey, Denon?" He wagged his head. I sat down next to him. "Hockey is a game played on ice. Do you know ice?" Again, he wagged his head. "Ice is water that is made so cold it becomes hard as this brick." His eyes widened a bit in disbelief. More *Mzungu* nonsense. "When the water turns to ice, we say it is 'frozen.' Can you say frozen?"

"Frosa?"

"That's good," I said. "Do you know when it is cold at night and you need a blanket to keep warm?" He nodded. "It must be much colder than that to make water turn into ice. You would need maybe ten blankets if it was that cold. There are whole cities in America where, in the winter, the water in rivers and lakes becomes frozen hard like this brick."

Denon stared at me with big curious eyes, eyebrows raised, silently processing.

"And when water is frozen, it becomes slippery. If you have special shoes called skates, you can move very fast over the ice. So people made up a game... a lot like your football except instead of a ball, they use a hard black piece of rubber called a 'puck.' Instead of their feet, they move the puck with sticks. And they move around on these skates. The object of the game is to get the puck into the goal – like football.

"Do you think you would like to play hockey someday, Denon?"

He thought a moment. "No, suh," he replied. "Not if I have to wear ten blankets."

The culture of hospitality in this place takes Western visitors by surprise at first, but very quickly becomes a lesson for how pleasant it is to experience welcome and unencumbered kindness. Here are some examples: When visitors are present, everyone in the room, no matter what age, introduces him or herself to every visitor. Whenever there is a meeting or a gathering, even in the poorest of places, there is food. Sometimes it is only tea, but here tea is not just a wet bag in hot water. Tea comes with two types of sugar and hot milk to accommodate anyone who wants to make "American tea," which is the wet bag in hot water, "English tea" which is hot tea with milk, or "African tea" which is mostly warm milk with spoonfuls of unrefined sugar, a bit of brewed tea and a touch of cinnamon. If the gathering is in the afternoon, there will likely be bread, boiled eggs and fresh fruit. If the gathering is in the evening, there will likely be a meal of rice, potatoes, peas and boiled beef. If the host wants to particular honor his guests, the meat will be roasted goat. Many times when telling friends that I will arrive on a certain date, they will say "That is wonderful. We will kill the goat for you."

It isn't until much later that you realize the food you are being served is much better than what the family might normally eat. Up country, an egg is precious and rare. To have a whole bowl of them hard boiled for visitors is like offering treasure. Likewise, most households do not eat meat at every meal or even every week. Cattle and goats and chickens often comprise the wealth of the household and people do not squander it lightly. But for visitors, they give it up without hesitation.

This sense of hospitality seems to be common to rural, third-world places. I remember being in a tiny village called *El Milagro* as part of a medical mission in the foothills of the Andes in Peru. When it came time for lunch, we were served delicious potatoes and vegetables and chicken. Whenever a plate was cleaned, it was immediately replenished, embarrassingly so, until we realized that if we were finished, we should leave something on the plate to so signify. It wasn't until later that we were told the family of five had not eaten chicken for a month – they had been purposefully and joyfully saving their animals for the missionaries as their way to pay for services rendered. I experienced the same dynamic in rural Southern Mexico, in a tucked away village in Honduras and in a tiny Christian Church near the Suez Canal in Egypt.

If we were on a path in Uganda and even hinted that we were not clear on our destination, children would appear and take us by the hand. If we arrived at a village with equipment that needed to be hauled, people would grab it without asking and carry it for us. We once brought a very heavy gasoline powered generator in our van. Two grownup American men would have struggled to carry the thing fifty feet but two skinny local kids about twelve years old picked it up and ran with it a quarter mile to the meeting site.

One doesn't need to be in country long before someone is calling you "Uncle or Auntie." Perhaps this comes from centuries of people living with enormous extended families, but it is culturally intimate and heartwarming to be genuinely considered a relative of someone you have known for only a week. I remember when Oprah Winfrey opened her Learning Center in South Africa, she had tears streaming down her face as the girls called her "Mam' Oprah." To this day, she speaks of the girls in that school as her children. Clearly, this custom gives meaning to the idea that "we are one body in Christ – all brothers and sisters in Him." In the case of Americans visiting Uganda, it isn't long before people are calling each other "Maama Clara, Auntie Barbara, Grandma Sandra, Uncle Bob or Bob-u" because such a simple way of expressing familiarity – as we often experience in our own extended families – bringing others into that close circle of trust and familiarity simply feels good to give and receive.

When I first heard the term "*Mzee*," it was applied to an older man in our group with white hair and a white beard because, in the local language the word means "respected elder." When the Africans said the word, they merged the M and the Z into 'm-ZAY' When Glen said it of himself, he said "MO-zay" which I thought at first was the local iteration of the name Moses. I embarrassed myself one day when I was introduced to a young *boda boda* driver whose name actually was Moses and, trying out the local language, I called him Mozay.

Everyone around this young man burst into howls of laughter at the name because they knew that there was no way this young guy was a respected elder.

I next was surprised to hear the term when Ben referred to His Excellency, the President of the country as Mzee and the First Lady as Maama. How amazing is this, I thought, that a citizen of the country feels close enough to its leaders to give them such warm, intimate labels. Then I heard Ben speaking of his father to his children. Everyone has pet names for Grandpa. In this case, Ben's dad was Mzee Mzee, the super-respected elder.

And so it is, over the years, as men older than Ben visit Uganda, they often walk away with the title Mzee. We have Mzee Glen *Wakazi*, the original American Mzee. We have Mzee George who is an Anglican pastor in the U.S. We have Mzee Bob *Agaba*, a man who has led young people on cross-cultural wilderness excursions for 20 years. And I am Mzee Lee *Twesigye* (trust in God). I am also called *Nshwento* (Uncle) by one of my young friends for whom Ben is a blood-relative uncle and *Taata* (Father or Dad) by some young people I have sponsored through school.

Ugandan hospitality goes even deeper when visitors are given an African name. The people here believe there is power in a name. It is tradition for fathers to name their children with hopeful middle names or even surnames such as *Nikirungi* (everything's fine) or *Mugisha* (blessed). Thus it is a bit of surprise that, once the Ugandan gets to experience a visitor in a variety of situations, very often and very casually, he might turn to that person and say, "You know, you are *Kiconco* (a gift)." And from that time on, that is how you are addressed.

To us, he is saying, to me you are no longer just Cathy, you are a gift from God and a blessing to me, *Kiconco*.

It is an odd feeling taking on a new name in this place. On one hand, you feel as though you are out of control, being drawn into a society before you're ready, becoming far too intimate with people you really don't know very well. On the other hand, it is extremely flattering because you realize the name they have given you is appropriate for you, sometimes far more apt than even you realize. You realize someone has been listening to you, watching you, reading you well below the surface, thinking about the exact word that portrays your real essence. Names are not given lightly. Sometimes they are not given at all. Sometimes it takes multiple visits before a name is bestowed because some people are harder to read than others and the Ugandans want to get it right. The names are always positive. When the name comes it must be right because it is an equalizing gesture, another sign of acceptance into the family. Sometimes the names are a surprise as though people never thought of themselves as being... a gift or a respected elder. We think about the names we have been given and why they were bestowed. There is never an explanation but we seek the rationale and ultimately devise our own, essentially forming ourselves into this vision someone else has of us – a positive influence, a confident being, a blessing, a person who is more spiritual than one realized. In the end, there is always this sense of wonder that people can know you for such a short time but can know you so well.

A young woman who was one of Ben's first guests to Uganda was called *Butesi* (One pampered by God) and ultimately became an ordained Anglican priest. A grandma was called *Arinaitwe* (God is with us) because she was the prayer warrior, ultimately fulfilling that position on Ben's U.S. Board of Directors. An outspoken female pastor, an ordained Canon of the church was called *Watamagongo* (a sort of mountain howitzer) because, being a Canon in the church, she boomed her guns of righteousness from the pulpit. A gentle young man with a knack for making friends of everyone he met was called simply *Rukundo* (love). A woman who braved a several long, arduous days with grace and humor was called *Ekoma* (steel). The leader of a mission team was called *Agaba* (God gives) after he led Bible studies on the side of a mountain in the dewy dawn. A college-aged woman thinking about becoming a full-time missionary was called *Tumukunde* (Let us love heaven). She returned to the U.S. and transferred from a secular college to a Christian one. A young man, a reluctant Christian, was named *Nemaata* (Sufficient for God), but after a camping experience with many rainy days, received a second name *Ruhumba Obwegyura* (He who lights a fire in the rain) because, with great dogged determination, he somehow kept the campfire alive even though all the available wood was wet. From the African point of view, this name was a metaphor for a courageous life. For the young man, the name became profound when he realized others recognized more inner strength in him than he realized in himself.

The name game goes both ways. If the Africans can give Americans names that reveal their impressions of us, we can do the same. Mark Twain realized this trekking across the desert in *Innocents Abroad* where, being unable to either pronounce or remember their names, called all local Arab guides Ferguson purely for his own convenience. We were sitting in Ben's house in Kishanje one evening while a local young man named Geoffrey strung wire and tiny bulbs across the ceiling in hopes of bringing electric light to the room from a car battery. He was splicing above our heads when sparks shot out and across the table. "Okay," someone said. "Your name is Sparky." Years later, Geoffrey is still known in the village as Sparky. Though it lacks something in metaphor, it carries the same intimacy of strangers loving each other.

What do we do with such lessons in hospitality? This question is one of the pieces of luggage we take home with us and, all too often, is never fully unpacked.

# A Spot of Land

*"Look to your left. The forest is still here."*
- A voice

I had a spot of land in Uganda high on a hill overlooking a deep, green corduroy valley at a place called Kishanje. From my plot I could see the lake, an iridescent blue gem shining at the end of great patchwork mounds. Some afternoons the clouds would settle between the hills like a mother hen covering her nest. Sometimes the clouds would darken and rumble and ignite deep inside and a curtain of gray rain would sweep up the valley toward me. A tiny forest of eucalyptus trees thirty feet tall covered one corner of the plot. This was unusual in an area where trees are cut for firewood, tools or building materials when they are ten feet tall. The trees marked the plot and made it visible from anywhere in the valley.

Standing there in the crystalline air with the little shouts and cries and clangs of village life echoing softly off the hills, I tried to imagine what it would be like to build a house and live in this place. I could retire here. Solar power. Captured rainwater. Organic food. A fireplace for chilly nights. House help. Room for visiting missionaries. But the dream bubble burst when I realized that no matter how much I tried, no matter how much I learned the language or history, no matter my level of hospitality or kindness or teaching of skills, I would always be known as "the *Mzungu*," and would never really be a part of the community. Nonetheless, I loved that patch of land and named it *Tierra Bendiga* – blessed land – in a language the local people would never understand.

Smitten with the area on my first trip to Africa, I had asked Ben, "What would it take to buy some lake property?"

"You can do that, Mzee" he said. "I can have my father ask around."

"Is it expensive?" I asked, having no idea about the cost of land anywhere on the continent.

"Lake land is less expensive than farm land."

"Really?"

"Yes, because it is not so good for farming. You get good drainage on the hills but at the lake the land is flat. Also people like living on the hills because they feel safer."

"But it is lake frontage. You know that people in the U.S. pay enormous amounts of extra money to live on the water."

"Yes, but here people do not like the water. They do not swim. The water is good – no crocodiles or hippos or Bilharzia – you know Bilharzia?"

"No."

"That is a fresh-water parasite that comes when people use the water for a latrine. The bug penetrates the skin and gets into the urinary system and causes lots of pain. We know this because people in other places wade into rivers and lakes to pee and they get sick. It is said to be quite agonizing. But this lake is clean. Nevertheless, people do not swim here because the banks are steep and many parts of the shore are marshy. It is hard for people to learn how to swim so they don't."

"Maybe we should look at buying land here," I mused.

A few months after I returned home, Ben called to say he had found a parcel of about four acres, up the hill from his house. "You wanted a plot with a view, Mzee. This is it. If you want it, send $2,500.00 before the end of the week."

I trusted Ben. I sent the money. What *Mzungu* in his right mind would buy a plot of land in an inaccessible part of the world sight unseen? Yes, I trusted Ben, but I felt secretly foolish and, for several years, never told my wife or anyone else about it.

By the time I returned to the land in Kishanje seven months later, the banana trees that were tall and spindly had yielded their fruit and had begun to wither. The eucalyptus were bigger. I walked the perimeter noticing weedless footpaths, shortcuts that criss-crossed the plot. Land might belong to someone, but clearly the community had access. Ben found me there one day. "Mzee, I have a favor to ask."

"You may have it," I replied.

"Wait. Let me tell you. It is my father, your *Shwenkulu* . He asks if he can plant beans on this plot while you are not using it."

I knew Ben's dad, David, having told him some years earlier that I had adopted him as my *Shwenkulu* or grandfather. For more than seventy years, David trod the steep hills of Kishanje in his worn tweed sport coat raising goats, growing beans, outliving wives and having children as his father did before him and his father before him.

I once asked Ben how old his father was and discovered nobody knew for sure. Age is irrelevant in this place because many older people in the villages have no idea when they were born because birth dates were never recorded. David was one of those. Having a child, raising the child, having the child take over the work, expecting the child to take care of you in your old age was just the rhythm of life. Time is measured by the rising and setting of the sun and in the growing seasons of yams or beans or potatoes, not in hours or days or dates. Many people cannot count, so counting years isn't done. Recently, when one grandma was asked how old she was, she replied, "seven." Young people around her howled with laughter because this woman was eighty if she was a day. She chuckled embarrassedly, for she didn't know one number from another and she certainly didn't know how old she really was, yet she, like David, had learned a smattering of English and thought she'd try it out.

David was born sometime in the 1920s during a long period of disease and famine, still recalled as "the bad times." People worked hard and struggled as they do today, but without rain the crops could not be coaxed from the ground and people starved. Of all his siblings, David is the only male who survived. The times were so difficult, David's father expressed his frustration and powerlessness when he named his son *Nshakabyanga* which means, "I struggle to succeed and feed my family but I fail. All the time." David was a young boy when his mother died and, shortly thereafter, his father died. A local sub-county government official took him in to be raised with his own family, a blessing to be sure, but when David graduated from his second year of primary school, his formal education ended; there was work to be done. The years of his youth passed quickly as David did various odd jobs to contribute to the household. However, during the second World War, when the British governor commanded that each family provide one male between the ages of 15 and 20 to be recruited into the King's African Rifles, David's foster father volunteered him for conscription.

The British were very practical in dealing with squabbles within their territories in that they used Africans from one business entity to reinforce Africans in other business entities that may be under threat or peril. From 1941 to 1952, some 44 battalions of the King's African Rifles fought in Abyssinia (Ethiopia) to repel an invasion of Italians; they wrested Madagascar from the Vichy French in 1942 to prevent the Japanese from building a submarine base; they fought in Burma in 1944 and helped quell the Mau Mau Rebellion in Kenya in 1952.[14]

David was sent to Nairobi to guard captured Italian prisoners of war. One day, with Ben translating, I asked him, "How long were you in the African Rifles?"

"Three years and three months," he replied. The story continued: after the war, David worked on a tea plantation in Tororo as the personal guard for the *Mzungu* manager. Later, he worked as a laborer in Buganda, now known as the capital city of Kampala. He then married and moved back to Kishanje, assuming the government position of "Area Manager" and had seven children. After twelve years in leadership, he went back to his fields of beans and his herds of goats. When his wife became ill, he married again while still caring for the first wife, and had nine more children. The first wife died in 1985. Later, he took a third wife and had three children by her. However, when he accepted Jesus Christ as his Lord and Savior in 1990, he wanted to be married in a church, but he realized having multiple wives was against the teachings of his

---

14    www.rhino-c link.co.uk/history_KAR.htm

new Lord Jesus so he convinced the youngest wife to return to her family in Fort Portal.

When Ben was young, he spent his days attending the local government-run primary school and herding goats. "I wanted to goof off like the other kids," he said. "But my father forced me to pay attention to school, often with persuasion administered to the seat of my pants."

Later, when it was time to go to secondary school, *Shwenkulu* had very little money, but he invested it all in his son's schooling. Early in the morning at the beginning of the school term, he would watch the boy traipse down the crooked path toward the lake with books and sleeping pad on his head. He knew Ben would find a dugout canoe waiting at the water's edge and would paddle a half hour across to the other shore. The boy would then walk four miles over steep hills to the school in Kabale town. Two or three times during the school term, late in the day and often after dark, his son would arrive home again, his arms full of books. He remembers Ben absorbed in his books, reading by the flames of the cooking fire, until he fell asleep, the open volumes on his chest. Ben told his dad how hard it was to study, how he would leave campus at night to go the local petrol station and read because that was the only building with electric lights burning late into the evening.

When I asked David if he ever went to a parent-teacher conference, he wrinkled his forehead trying to decipher the meaning of the words. The only interaction he had with school was receiving a piece of paper once in awhile with writing on it. A report card. Typed in opaque purple ink on "flimsy" with letters and numbers he couldn't read.

Ben did so well in school he earned a government scholarship to Makerere University in Kampala. He became a political activist on campus and, in his Junior year, caused a riot protesting the rule of dictator Milton Obote at which he was arrested and put in jail. It was there, reading through a castoff Bible that Ben dedicated his life to God's work by making the prisoner's bargain: "God, if you let me go free, I will be your steadfast servant forever." His fear was real because it was common during this time that people had been exiled to prison or executed for lesser offenses. But the next day, and Ben insists it was by the grace of God, his case was dismissed. He has been God's steadfast servant ever since.

When Ben graduated from university, David gave his son a small plot of land and a cow. The land had a large eucalyptus tree on it. In this village, the greatest gift one generation can bestow on another is land because tilling the earth yields food and sustains life. To give up a piece of land is akin to giving away the future of your family. It is your retirement, your investment portfolio and your savings account all rolled into one. You do it only when you are sure it will be used wisely.

No longer a student, Ben needed a house, so he began working the soil from his land into bricks. Day by day, he graded the land by shovel and hoe into a flat space, mixing clay soil with water and placing the mud into forms. Once dried in the sun, the bricks were piled up into the shape of a flat-topped pyramid, leaving a cavity in the center with a small access hole to the outside. The pile, about 12 feet high, was covered with green grass and soil. Then a fire was built in the cavity and stoked from time to time. Over a period of weeks, the fire cooked the entire pile, turning the adobe block into weather-proof building brick.

Meanwhile, Ben cut the tree to use for building supports. He sold the cow to buy metal doors, window guards and roofing sheets. In time, Ben turned the bequest from his father into a permanent house just up the hill from where he was born.

During his 10 years working at Scripture Union, Ben would visit his little house and find peace. Eventually, he applied for and won a Billy Graham scholarship to Wheaton College in America where he earned a Master's Degree. But he regularly returned to Uganda, to his little house in the hills, to remember his promise to God. He married and returned to America and earned a second Master's degree at Trinity International University. His wife, Lilian, earned a degree in sewing and drapery design. They had two children. In 2001, he began bringing Americans to Uganda to visit his village and hosted people in his little house. When Ben and Lilian and the American-born kids moved back to Uganda in 2005, he added more rooms. It became a part-time school and the pivot point for ministry work done throughout the district. You'll read more about that later.

While Ben was away in America at the dawn of a new century, David trod the hills of Kishanje in British army boots working to put food on his family's table. He watched with pride and amazement as his son brought small groups of Americans to this remote speck of Africa. He strove to learn English in order to speak to these people. He acquired a cell phone to be in touch with his family. If you asked him, he would tell you the latest years of his life were the most productive. Mzee David's integral role in the village led to the acquisition of the plot of land where he now wanted to plant beans.

My answer to Ben's question was "Of course *Shwenkulu* may plant beans on this land. And may the harvest be bountiful. But Ben," I asked. "I have seen no paperwork on this plot. How do I know I own it?"

"You do, Mzee. I have a receipt for the money from the man who sold it to you."

"Don't you think we should get a survey and a title to prove ownership?"

"You could do those things. We would have a surveyor come from Mbarara. He would measure and make a plat. We could take that to Kabale town and register it and receive a deed. It would cost money and take a year or two. But Mzee, you would be the first one in Kishanje to do such a thing."

Ben smiled at the question mark on my face.

"People here know who owns what," he said. "They know who used to own what. They know how parcels are divided among children. It is a known thing. It is not written down because, remember, Mzee, most people here cannot read or write. Nevertheless, they know about property and they respect each other's rights. If there was ever a dispute, the town elders would only ask several people to recall the facts. But there are no disputes. Because everyone knows."

"If I wanted to sell..."

"...Word goes out among the people that a parcel is for sale. A price is agreed upon. You would get your money. You would give the buyer a piece of paper – a receipt for the transaction. And everyone would know. You want to sell? You would make some money."

"No," I replied quickly. "This is *Tierra Bendiga*."

"It is a known thing. Nothing is written," he said. The words stuck in my head for days. I had noticed people in church, reciting the Book of Romans from memory. The pastor would choose a hymn and the congregation would know all the verses by heart. There were stories of elders in the tribes and villages who told stories to the young. These were the historians passing lore and lessons to the next generation.

"It is one of the great tragedies of the AIDS era," said Rev. Benoni Mugarura in Kampala. "We lost the generation of people who would have told the stories to their children. When the old people die without passing on the lore with the lessons and the customs, the reasons behind the rules, the standards, it is like an entire library has burned to the ground. A village's identity – its recorded ancestry - is lost."

I recognized the sad reality, but at the same time, I saw tribal Africans in a new light. These were highly intelligent people who had laws and lore and history and a proven means for passing it on. The process of passing it on tied old to young, created respect, maintained order and a trustworthy sense of family continuity. Of course I had read Alex Haley's *Roots* where he idealized tribal life in Africa with its rituals of manhood and rigid sense of hierarchy, a pattern of life too often destroyed by the Arabic slavers. But maybe it wasn't so idealized after all.

The villages had evolved over hundreds, maybe thousands of years, living according to a set of rules that ensured their survival. It wasn't that long ago – well into the 1950s that a young girl who became pregnant before marriage was banished from the village. It was the custom that girls were raised to be pure at marriage and then faithful to one man until death. This custom created a predictable sense of order in village life. Any deviation was dealt with seriously.

A boy who made an unmarried girl pregnant would be chased by her brothers with spears until he was killed or driven permanently away from the village. In the Kishanje area, the girl would be taken to a place called Punishment Island in the middle of Lake Bunyoni and left there to starve to death. To Westerners, this may seem like a harsh tradition, but evolution and tribal experience had proven over the ages that children from unmarried couples could not assimilate into families; the customs of inheritance were upset; there was no clear family hierarchy for establishing order; the rites of passage would be denied to bastard children for there could be no joy in the family if a child did not belong to the family. Bastard children led to a weak society and a weak society in ancient tribal Africa meant death to a village.

On one of his fundraising trips to the U.S., some three years after Mzee David planted his beans, Ben approached me. "Mzee, I want to build on your land. You have seen the work that is going on there. I want to build the Kishanje Learning Advancement Center on that plot."

His words hit me like a brick. I supposed at some point in time we would use the land for building, but for some reason, the request bothered me. I now know why. *Tierra Bendiga* was part of a place where life is uncomplicated. People work hard. They feed themselves. They live with only the seasons to remind them of the passage of time. They are a village where everyone is known. There is little or no crime. Living in big families, children must learn to fend for themselves early on. Without electricity, there are few distractions – no machines, no TV, no Game Boy, no Internet. Living in clean air, drinking clean water, eating organic grains, fruits and vegetables and walking the hills, people are strong and healthy, often living into their nineties. They are not obsessed with health care; if someone gets sick, they either get better or they die. Children are born, they grow into adults and when they get old, their children take care of them. It is a rhythm of life that was uninterrupted for hundreds of years. It was simple. Beautiful. So different from the West. I didn't want to be a part of anything that would break the rhythm.

But, of course, the AIDS epidemic already did that.

You'll read a lot about the AIDS epidemic as you persevere with this book, but let me just say that, in the span of 20 years, an entire generation between the young and the old was swept away by disease. Suddenly the grandmas, at an age where their children should be taking care of them, were taking care of their children's children. The rhythm had been upset for an entire generation.

It was this reality that caused us to begin caring for AIDS orphans in the first place. Six months after Ben launched his ministry called Juna Amagara (which means "Saving Life" in the local language), I traveled with Ben and a group of Americans to his village. It was after dark when we arrived at Kishanje, but the sound of a van on the road and the mere presence of headlights signaled our arrival to people for miles around. In the morning, quiet murmurs woke us from sleep. We heard the shuffling of bare feet on earth outside our window. One by one, we roused out of our bunks to see what was happening. The sight that greeted us in the new morning sun broke our hearts. There, in line at the door, were the grandmas, two dozen of them, each with a child or two, some with babies in their arms. Ben spoke to them gently in *Rukiga* and then came into the house with tears streaming down his face.

He explained: "They heard us arrive last night. They know we have started a ministry to take care of orphans. They came today to give us their children."

The only sound in the room was profound silence, eleven souls rapt in the reality of drowning people begging for a lifeline. And we had none. We all had tears in our eyes. "I had to tell them we cannot take their children," Ben said. "We have no money. We have no place to house them. We have only started. We can only promise that we will do something. I told them God would hear their prayers, but I had to turn them away," he said. This was the only time I ever saw the lips tremble on his strong, round face. Outside, the old women walked away up the road, a little more bent, holding children by the hand or tightening the infants in a sash on the back. Their dresses were explosive in joyous color but their bright hopes had been ground into the earth. They would deal with it. They would survive as they always had. They would do as their neighbor son had said and ask God to take care of them... again.

Just two years after we turned the grandmas away, in the same place with the same weathered faces and many of the same children, hope and joy had replaced despair. More than 100 children had been brought into a new Juna Amagara program which meant money provided by child sponsors in the US was used to help the Grandmas be better guardians of the children and also provided badly needed supplemental education. Ben instructed a young Kishanje man named Moses to start a tutoring program where kids would show up at Ben's house after school to get help with homework and learn things about their subjects not taught in school, something guardians who could not read English and who never went to school could not do. In public school classes sometimes with more than 50 kids, individualized learning was nonexistent. Thus, working with these kids after school was the only way to help them excel and pass the tests they needed to go on to higher grades. Besides tutoring, the children were each fed a hot meal. Every day. A hundred kids. The teachers worked with marker boards tacked to trees. Reading lessons took place in the grass, Bible studies on the stoop. One small bedroom held three treadle-powered sewing machines and a knitting machine where young women learned to sew. When it rained, class was over.

The tutoring program had been in place for six months by the time I saw it. Yet, the difference in the children was astounding. Dull eyes, runny noses, and slouchy standing around had turned into bright faces, vibrant smiles and energetic dancing. We learned that the tutored kids regularly took their newfound knowledge home where they helped siblings with their homework by candle light. We learned they were at the heads of their classes in public school, often teaching the teachers. They told Bible stories to their guardians. The grandmas told how the kids now behave so much better: "Their minds are engaged," they said. "The children have no time for the mischief idleness breeds."

The Grandmas themselves were also transformed. Before AIDS, before the soldiers, before independence, more than 40 years ago, the women of this region were renowned for their weaving. They would use local materials – bamboo, papyrus, raffia and buffalo grass to make baskets with striking designs and colors. They wove mats for the floors of their huts. Eating mats. Door mats. Window coverings. They made intricately woven baskets – small and large, with lids and handles. But the "bad times" had drained their energy and the weaving stopped.

Until this day.

The weight of survival had eased enough that some women who remembered their weaving skills began to teach others. Soon there were a dozen weavers. They began to meet often to share skills, to talk about their children, to gossip and laugh while they wove and suddenly a neighborhood orphan care support group was born. The weaving was not of great quality... yet. But in the mood, you could feel the hope and in the working fingers, see the joy.

This was progress, a return to the rhythm of life. An answer to prayers.

"We need a place to tutor these kids where they can work when it rains," Ben said. We need space for the women to sew. We need a library and a computer center. This is what we need to build."

"Would this Kishanje Learning Advancement Center take up the whole plot?" I asked.

"No, no, Mzee, only about a third. You would still have room to build your bungalow." He had read my mind. I did not want the fantasy of living here with this view out my back window to die. "Here, I have a diagram." He showed me a piece of paper with kindergarten squares drawn on it indicating rooms marked with slashes for doors and windows. "We can save lots of money – we just take the plan that was drawn for the children's home we completed last year and modify it. No problem."

I had seen the results of "No problem" already in Africa. Houses cobbled together with leftover scraps of wood and

corrugated cartons, makeshift roof beams that attacked anyone over five feet tall, cooking on wood fires indoors with no
chimney. The children's home he spoke of was only a quarter
the size and a different shape than the building he proposed.

"Ben, this is too rough. You need to get an architect to visit
the site and draw a plan."

"No, No, Mzee, I must insist! We need to get going now.
You will see. We can modify the other plan."

"Sorry, Ben, but I must insist. The other site was flat. This
is sloped. You had one building before. This is two or more.
This is a different size. Your drawing has three doors for one
room. Please get a plan."

He threw up his hands in surrender. "If I get a plan can we
build on your land?"

"Of course," I said, knowing at last why I bought the plot
in the first place. "But, my brother," I added. "There is a small
eucalyptus forest on the land. You must promise me the trees
will not be cut." He assured me the trees would be there when
I visited the parcel on my next trip. With that promise, I
believed the land would begin to live up to its name. And if it
caused a ripple in the time warp between modern society and
this isolated rural culture, I could only hope that the lives of
the people in the area would be enriched by the children who
would cause the change.

Ben returned to Uganda focused on finding an architect. A
month later, we received photos of Ben with his father, David,
wielding a heavy farming hoe, breaking ground for the first
foundation.

A few months later, I visited my little spot of land. When
I climbed the hill and saw the site, I could only stare word-
lessly at what I found. It was the same inspired sensation I

had when I came upon Machu Picchu at sunrise. What a wonder the people had wrought out of the terraced hillside.

Two classrooms were completed and under roof. The walls
for two others were ready for rafters. Another two rooms were
waiting for the ring beam. The foundation for the main building had been dug, half of it lined with a concrete footing. More
than 100 people, all locals, swarmed over the site carrying
bricks on their heads, carrying mortar pans made out of the
lids of 55-gallon drums on their heads, carrying water jugs
on their heads, mixing mortar, laying bricks, building forms,
using mattocks to sculpt the earth. There wasn't a power tool
within three hours driving time from this site, yet the walls
were rising strong and straight from the earth before my eyes.

The plot looked so different from the last time I saw it. I
searched around trying to get my bearings... the footpath off
the main road was still there next to the trees. The trees. What
happened to my eucalyptus forest? I ran up the hill to find
stumps where two-thirds of the forest had been hacked down –
some of the biggest trees. I could feel the anger welling up.
"He promised me the forest would be here when I returned," I
muttered. "These people have no sense of how they are defil-
ing their own land," I cursed. And then a little voice made
itself heard inside my head. It was gentle. Calm. It said, "The
forest is still here. Look to your left." When I did, I saw the
bustle of people carrying, digging and building. Then I looked
closer. The eucalyptus trees were there, only they had become
scaffolding, braces and ladders. Large trees were sawn into
boards to make concrete forms. Edge pieces formed bridges
over open foundations, shortening the distances for barefooted workers with wheelbarrows.

Then the voice said, "You can plant more trees."

I had not uttered a word of my disappointment, but no more than twenty minutes later, young Moses Mwesigye came up to me and said, "Mzee, you wanted to plant some trees? There is a place not far from here where they have eucalyptus seedlings. We can go today if you want." God got me again.

Two days later we took the truck, found the nursery and bought 100 eucalyptus seedlings for 5,000 Ugandan shillings – the equivalent of about $3.00. We brought them back and formed a team of volunteers who labored on the hillside for an afternoon digging holes and planting trees. Even as the seedlings were settling into their new earth, we noticed the stumps of hacked-off trees putting out shoots to grow new trees. I could envision that a year later, the hill will be full of trees. In ten years, maybe less, the forest will be thick and strong once again.

When we were finished, the planting team gathered in prayer. "Dear Father God," I murmured. "I am so humbled. I am ashamed that I doubted your plan for this place. I am inspired and amazed at the way you answer so many prayers and shower so many blessings in such elegant ways. Just... when I get pissed off for my own petty reasons, please be patient with me – as you have in this case – and help me realize again and again, you really do have it all figured out and you really are in control after all. Amen."

As the days unfolded, the miracle of this place became more evident. By undertaking a large building project and using local people to do the building, Ben transformed the community. Where six months before, the women would spend their days puttering in the fields and the men would go to the bars because they had nothing else to do, now they worked here and earned badly needed wages. The bars were virtually empty. The crops were still well tended.

New skills were being taught and applied. I met two women who learned to make bricks at the KLAC site. One of them named Charity was 19 years old. As the oldest of five children without parents, she was the head of their household. Just the memory of this woman singing in church brings goose bumps to my arms, a high, clear, powerful voice filling the building and anchoring a hundred other voices along the way. She put that same power to work on the job site humming, swinging, swaying with a trowel in her hand. You could feel her joy. With the money she earned laying bricks, she could now afford to send all of her siblings to school.

American father-and-son electricians visited the site to install boxes and conduit that will one day hold wiring for lights and outlets. Along with the work, they taught two local young men how to be electricians. After two weeks working side by side with the Americans, young Moses and Charles had gained the skills to finish wiring the buildings. There is no public electric utility in Kishanje, so innovative technologies are being applied to harness both wind and solar power for the complex. When completed, the facility will have lighting in all rooms, a computer lab and a library.

The project has singlehandedly created a local building supplies industry. Bricks are being made locally. Stone for foundations and mortar is quarried locally. Sand for mortar has been found locally. On roads within five miles of the project, one finds piles of bricks or stone ready to sell, a phenomenon that did not exist six months earlier. All of this has not only brought revenue to people desperately short of cash, but it has allowed Juna Amagara to build at far less cost than anticipated. The community is proud that such a building is rising out of the earth. It is their project for their children built with their sweat from their soil. It is no wonder singing bursts out spontaneously with energy and harmony one only finds in Africa.

Ben organized a ceremony to commemorate the formal transfer of the land from my hands to the ministry. As usual, the man organized big. He ferried a team from Life Ministries from Mbarara along with several cases of sound equipment, projection equipment, loud speakers, a generator and a portable movie screen. When the crew arrived on Saturday night before the ceremony, they played Ugandan pop-Christian-rock *Beera Nange* over the big speakers and people from throughout the district danced well into the night.

After church on Sunday, the celebration crew set up their generator and microphones on the site of the Kishanje Learning Advancement Center. By the time the program began, more than 400 people crowded there along with pastors, village leaders, visitors from the U.S., a local member of parliament and a camera man from Uganda Broadcasting. Ben's dad was there in a natty gray suit, crisp white shirt, red tie and shiny Oxfords. The pastors prayed. The politicians made speeches. Ben preached to the crowd, mostly in *Rukiga*.

Then, in English, he said, "I have been telling people that Jesus called his disciples together and gave them new names. He wanted to commission them as new workers with a new task. The history of my father's family is that my grandfather struggled to find food and some of my father's siblings died because of starvation. My father is the only male who survived out of my grandfather's progeny and the name he was given, *Nshakabyanga*, conveyed that reality. My grandfather said 'I try my best to search for goods, to search for food to feed my family and I fail. All the time. My father was given that name. Then my grandfather died. Then my grandmother died, leaving my father an orphan. My father was taken care of by a government official who was compassionate enough to take him in. That's why we are taking care of orphans. We are giving back. But my father was never given an education. That's why we are building a Learning Advancement Center so that the children here will be given a good education. So, today, I have given my father a new name. It is *Nshakabyingi,* which means 'I go to search and seek and I find plenty.' His named is changed today. In the sight of all these witnesses, people as old as he is, people who have known him all his life, we change his name. His children and his grandchildren and his great grandchildren must now call him by this name."

He asked his father to stand and he put his arm around the old man's shoulders. They hugged in a tearful embrace. It was the most moving tribute by a son to his father I have witnessed in my lifetime.

Then he asked me to stand while he read the letter of transferral. I am not used to being on the lens side of a camera and it was awkward for me, but Ben wanted to acknowledge the gift before the people of his village. Then he unveiled what he called a foundation stone – a permanent record of this day, honoring his father and Mzee Lee Twesigye for the land that was to become a school. Together, *Shwenkulu* and I spread mortar on the wall of the main building, next to the front door, and placed the stone for all to see. The cameras of Uganda Television whirred. Flashes popped. People clapped.

The wiry old African and I hugged as though we truly were father and son.

These things are all past tense because, six weeks after laying the foundation stone into the rough new walls of the Kishange Learning Advancement Center, David died. To me, he will always be *Shwenkulu,* the grandfather who invested his last dime in a boy with fire for knowledge in his heart and a mischievous twinkle in his eye. Everyone who traveled to Kishanje with Ben greeted David warmly but the old African and I wept with joy when we saw each other. We sang *tukutendereza* together. We patted each other on the back in the African way. On every trip to Uganda, I could hardly wait to see him again.

His body was buried on the side of a steep hill near his home in the same soil as his ancestors, his siblings, his wives and his children, the same soil that has sustained his people for a thousand years, the same soil from which a million bricks have been cast for a learning center that bears his name. I will really miss that guy.

*Tierra Bendiga* indeed.

# PART II

## The Reality
## of HIV/AIDS

*"For people in the West, AIDS is a distant theory, someone else's problem. But for us, AIDS is personal. We have all watched relatives wither and die. We have attended too many funerals."*

– Bishop Zac Nirungye

# They Died

*"Love your neighbors, but not to death."*
- Pastor Frank Isingoma

When you talk to people in Uganda about AIDS, you get used to hearing the words, "They died." I lost three sisters. They died. The person who was paying my school fees. He died. The people I knew in that town. They died. The man who was her boyfriend, he died, she died. You hear it so much, the words lose meaning. Yet every one of these deaths was preceded by long and painful suffering, a withering of the body and the spirit into oblivion. The anguish extends to the caregivers and the relatives, the friends, the villagers and the loved ones, not just as a relationally shared pain for the disease but also for the anxiety of 'who else is carrying the virus and am I next?' For those who have lost multiple family members or multiple neighbors in a village, the anguish is numbing. Dying is taken for granted. It is too normal. It happens too often.

And as sad as it is to lose people to disease, the true tragedy becomes clear in those people left behind, often children who have no means to support themselves.

On one of my first trips to Uganda, I stayed with Amos and Mabel Twinamasiko in their home in Mbarara. The house could be a modest home in suburban Florida, built of concrete-block-and-stucco painted pastel with a tile roof surrounded by a sedgy lawn and fruit trees. Dr. Amos is an ophthalmologist in the local hospital and over breakfast one morning, I asked about his family's encounter with AIDS. "Well," he began. "I came from a family of 10 of which only four of us are left. Mabel comes from family of nine of which only three are left. And for those who died, each left multiple children behind. We just buried a niece who had been recently married and left four kids."

"What happens to these children," I asked

"We try to take care of them," Dr. Amos said. I had heard this time and time again about Uganda: A million parents dead. A million and a half children cut off from their only means of food, shelter and care in a nation without a working public welfare system. Seven hundred thousand of these had been taken up by family, friends or caring people in the village. Ben had told me of the children he had supported through University including his nephew Herbert and this on his miniscule missionary's income. A woman known as Aunt Jocelyn, somewhat prosperous with shops and a farm, cares for multiple children in her home and employs them in her businesses. A prominent local women's rights consultant named Jolly Bibarikamu and her husband Erik reported raising and educating some 19 children to date through university level. "We ourselves currently support five kids with school fees," she said. "The number varies, but there are always four."

And what of the rest of the children?

"The rest," Dr. Amos said. Mabel turned her head to hide the tear welling in her eye. "The rest we pray for."[15]

We began to notice the orphans. There are children everywhere in Uganda, but it didn't take long before we could spot the lost ones standing in small clumps, watching but not seeing. One of our group, a grandmother named Jeanine, recalls, "We were driving back to town along a dirt road when I saw a little girl about eight with a baby strapped to her back. She was just walking. It was midnight. There were no grownups, certainly no parents around. I asked someone about her. They told me she was just looking for a place to sleep. I had come to Africa specifically to help the children, and here were two and we did not stop. That happened a lot."

Our team would finish its presentations to classes of fresh-faced students in crisp uniforms and invariably, walking out of the school, we would see clusters of children across the street, watching but not seeing. They were thin, dirty and barefoot, with runny noses, wearing mismatched clothes donated from somewhere in the US, now ragged, filthy and full of holes. Those children are still there today. They stand and stare for hours without expression, the eyes barely moving; someone called them the "ghost children. If you talk to them, they acknowledge you with a nod and if they speak, it is only a whisper. Younger kids cling to older kids. They are clearly hungry, unhealthy and depressed of spirit. We could not help but wonder if these were from child-headed families, where a 12 or 14 year-old might be the oldest of five siblings and therefore head of household. They scour the dumps for food. They work at menial jobs like breaking rocks or selling oranges or herding goats to earn a few shillings – 1,700

15    Interview, Amos and Mabel Twinamasiko in Mbarara January 23, 2005

shillings to the dollar – to buy a piece of bread to split four ways. Is it any wonder that any symbol of success here relates to food? Hospitality centers around meals, therefore prosperous people are fat. Can we ever be surprised that when a van load of Americans shows up, we should wonder why they think we are rich?

Even those in foster care – those lucky enough to be taken in by someone are not always better off. Coerced sexual liaisons are common as is The Cinderella Syndrome where orphans taken into a house with biological children present are treated as servants for the family – much like Ben's dad David experienced in his youth. Uncooperative children are beaten with sticks. From age 13, girls might survive under the care of "sugar daddies" in return for sexual favors. Orphan boys become "hooligans" meaning petty thieves and troublemakers. Anything to survive. Anything to go to school, to learn a skill, to live long enough to become an adult.

The words of Bishop Zac came home – in America we are not touched by AIDS; it *is* a distant theory. We were so ignorant. And so we asked questions:

"Ben, if the parents died of AIDS, do the children have the virus?"

"Some do but the vast majority do not. Certainly if the parents contracted the disease after children are born, the kids are OK. Infants born of infected parents can be HIV positive but with good food and care, they can outgrow it. Children who try to care for dying parents, with open sores are at risk because they will clean an open wound with bare hands. The parent's virus can enter any cut or abrasion on the hand and the disease will transfer."

"What is the life expectancy of a child with AIDS?"

"With good food and a healthy environment, some can live 18 or 25 years or more. If they get anti-retroviral drugs (ARV's), even longer; people now say a normal life expectancy.

"How many people have died of AIDS?"

"We really don't know," Ben said. "AIDS causes immune-deficiency so people can get malaria or influenza or other things and because they can't fight it, they die and it is attributed to that disease. Only blood tests will tell if it the death was related to AIDS and those tests are not generally done. But we know over a million parents have died leaving more than 1.5 million kids to fend for themselves."

What is the greatest challenge for child-headed families?" I asked.

"Food, of course," he said. "Young children work all day for one meal. And shelter. This is important because there are crazy grownups who try to take advantage of these kids – steal what little they have or attempt rape. Someone must always be on guard. These kids grow up tough and very few go to school.

In town after town, school after school, family after family, the depth of the sorrow of the tragedy of AIDS settled upon us. We stopped in an out-of-the-way village to check on the sister of William Asiimwe, a man who had been traveling with us for a week. Here was a young mother, suffering with AIDS and near death. The painfully emaciated figure lay in a fetal position on a blanket on the dirt floor in the corner of a windowless room. She could not speak and only nodded to her brother's questions. Amazingly calm and with smiling encouragement, William gently put a blanket over her. "This is the third sister I have lost," he said. Next door, a neighbor watched while the sister's two infant children played in the dirt with a half dozen other kids.

Our hearts broke that day and so, near the end of that first trip in November 2003, we sat with Ben and said, "You have told us you will be returning to Uganda once your schooling is finished. What do you want to do? We have seen the need. We are moved to tears. How can we help?" Without hesitation, he answered simply, "I want to give these orphan children a chance at life."

Once back in the U.S., we held a "re-entry" reunion for trip participants. It was a good thing we did because everyone in the group confessed a sense of depression upon coming home, something we each thought was unique to ourselves. Though we were glad to be back in the land of the clean bathroom, supermarkets, and streets without ruts, we could not shake the memories of children we had met, struggling to survive, grateful for the merest kindness in a society doing everything it can to help its own people but failing from lack of resources. We talked through these things and soon we were laughing through our tears. Someone brought a laptop and said half-seriously, "If we were going to start a ministry, what would it look like?" The PowerPoint screen was blank, but the ideas started to flow. An outline formed. A presentation was built with photos we had taken. The ministry would be a stool with three legs: First, we would have housing and caregivers to take in the neediest of the needy, children that have no hope and raise them as a family. Second, we would support orphan kids with school fees and vocational training in order to equip them to be productive adults. And third, we would evangelize, spread the lessons of Jesus and the love of God the Father to the youth of the region.

Ben and members of that mission team presented the vision for the work on January 11, 2004 to 55 people who had assembled in a Presbyterian Church parlor to hear the story. At the end, many of those people were moved to write checks and Juna Amagara Ministries was born. Six weeks later, the first Amagara Children's House was open in the town of Mbarara, staffed and equipped with the first 14 kids in residence. That was fast action by any standards, but for Americans used to being inherently skeptical that anyone in Africa really could do anything the American way, to say a the project was complete in that time was hard to believe. The lesson was clear: if the Ugandan people wanted this so badly and could execute so well, we reasoned, who were we to stand in the way?

A number of us returned to Uganda in June of 2004 to see just what it was the people of this tiny ministry had put together. We arrived in Mbarara town at lunch time and met over a meal where the noon buffet offered *chapati* and peas, *matooke* with peanut sauce, stewed brown meat, sliced tomatoes and spongy millet bread. Joining us was one of Ben's great friends, John Mulindabigwi who had been recruited to direct a steering committee for Juna Amagara activities in Mbarara. He told us something about the children. "We have gathered these kids from a variety of villages," he said. "Some we had known about for some time because we know people in all these places. Once we had the facilities ready Herbert Ainamani and I rented a van and, in one long day, gathered them up." John told of their travels over rutted roads that went well into the night. "Some of the guardians were waiting for us," he said. "The child would have a few belongings wrapped in a shirt and the other children would just watch him go away into this van with strangers. We picked one boy from a child-headed family. It would have been good to take all five but we could only take one. They hugged their brother and sadly watched him go. Another child came from a house where the mom had died and the dad was lying in the room close to death. One girl was picked from the home of the village leader after midnight where one candle lit the room. She had been delivered there by some people. And so it went."

John had met us with effusive greetings and an infectious smile. With a round face and small eyes, eyebrows perpetually raised in wonder, he spoke with a calm voice and a demeanor tempered by dealing with the adversity of people. Later we would learn John and his wife Jolly had six children and hosted so many people in their modest home, their neighbors thought he was running a hotel. As he told us the story of how he and Herbert gathered the children, the smile had long since disappeared. Wrinkles creased his brow when he described the blank looks on the faces of the children not taken and the stoic resignation of those chosen. "You need to know these things before you meet these kids," he said. "I will be interested to see your reaction."

Somebody paid the bill, we got back into the van and rode for fifteen minutes through the winding, Burma Road back streets of Mbarara, and then finally, turning down a tree-lined track and into a yard where a modest house painted pastel aqua, sat under a Ficus tree. Before the van stopped, the children came out to greet us. They ranged in age from six to 16 years. Bright-eyed, they introduced themselves in cautious, whispery voices. Some girls greeted us with curtseys. After John introduced us to them in *Rukiga,* they smiled luminous, perfect smiles and sang a short welcome song. The facilities were simple but adequate - wrought iron on the windows and doors, bunk beds, the traditional outdoor cooking shed, latrines, a garden. A fence of thorny bushes surrounded the property. We met the staff, a matron and a cook, young women fresh out of teacher's colleges. And then we were asked to sit on a bench while our children – they called them our children – sang for us.

Over the next hour, with only a drum for accompaniment, kids in smart red and blue school uniforms, all ages and sizes, sang in perfect harmony and danced in simple choreography for their guests. Having been in the U.S. while the program came together, Ben was seeing these children for the first time just as we were. He watched with tears streaming down his face when the children sang: "Things already bettah. Things already bettah. When the Lord is come we know things already bettah." Later, the children performed The Orphan Dance, a drama where they enacted the typical family scenario from the child's point of view: mom and dad die, the kids are stigmatized by peers and adults, someone offers a pencil as the symbol of education, someone gives them a hand up and the story ends in smiles.

When it was over, John Mulindabigwi said, "It is so wonderful to see these kids. You see their energy, the exercises they can do. They are smiling. You would almost not think these were the kids we picked just a few months ago. These ones will not become hooligans."

While these chosen children, a minute fraction of the orphan population of this district were wearing their school uniforms, singing and dancing and chatting with visitors, the others, the barefoot ones not included stood at the gate a short distance away like shadows, watching with dull eyes and runny noses, dressed in raggedy clothes, looking on not with envy but just knowing that whatever miracle had occurred, it had not included them. For them, death was not far away.

# The Clay Factory
# of Rakai

*"So this is how AIDS spreads? Clearly we don't have a medical problem. We have a behavior problem."*
- Yoweri Museveni, President of Uganda

On the way to Kishanje Village, I wanted to take a turn off the Mbarara road to travel through Rakai, a district on the shore of Lake Victoria. It was here that powerful Christian leaders Kay Warren of Saddleback Church and Rick Stearns, President of World Vision became tearfully "broken" when they met orphans in the huts and hovels of child-headed families here and inspired huge orphan ministries as a result.

Many local people I spoke to including two physicians agreed that it was here in the late 1970s that this was ground zero, the place where two Congolese fishermen infected with HIV came ashore and sparked a rampant epidemic. Though the disease existed elsewhere in the region, it was this place that marks the beginning of its wildfire spread throughout Africa.

Rakai was vibrant then, a popular stop on the freight route across southwest Uganda. Trucks laden with goods from the port of Mombasa in Kenya and manufactured goods from

Jinja would ride all day across the flat plain of the Great Rift Valley and stop for the night in towns here before completing journeys to Tanzania, Rwanda, Burundi or Eastern Congo. Every truck driver and passenger bus stopping in the towns of this district – Masaka, Lyantonde, Lukaya, Kinoni was like the prodigal ant being welcomed back into the colony. There were "hotels," mud-walled rooms with sleeping cots lit by the flame of a tea candle. There were densely packed bars where a man could get a warm Nile Extra Beer, a long story and a too-loud laugh. And there were women who would make themselves available to the drivers, the captains of 18-wheeled ships of the savannah for only a few shillings more than the beer. Little did any of the sex workers know that the fishermen who were also their customers had given them a deadly disease they would pass along, a biological time bomb whose devastation would not be known for years. The women gave it to the drivers. The drivers gave it to others along the route and their wives and girlfriends when they returned home and their girlfriends passed it to other lovers.

By the early 1980s, people throughout this district began wasting away. Then, as now, it was normal for people to have bouts of malaria or diarrhea or open cuts and sores, but in those days the sicknesses did not subside and wounds did not heal. People with minor ailments mysteriously withered and died from a condition they called "Slim."

Then, suddenly, it seemed everyone had the disease. No one knew where it came from. No one knew what caused it. Witch doctors blamed curses sent from Tanzania. Others blamed God for sending punishment for reasons known only to Him.

Dr. Phinehas Tukamuhaabwa, now a Professor in the Agriculture Department at Makerere University was a university student at the time. Between terms, he and scores of other students would ride the bus home for the holiday. The road from Kampala to Kabale town was not paved which meant the trip took two days, requiring an overnight stop. On the way home, the students, exhausted from exams, generally slept. But returning to school, rejuvenated with home cooking, plenty of sleep and some shillings in their pockets, they felt their oats. Phinehas recalls, "The boys would yell and jump and scream and try to make time with the girls. And when the bus stopped for the night at towns of Rakai, they went wild. They would go to the bars. They went off with the women.

"But some of us did not get off the bus," he said. "The others taunted us as cowards, calling us names. We ate food we had brought with us. We sang quiet songs together. We prayed all night.

"In the end," Phinehas said, "All the people who got off the bus died within a short time. Some before they graduated. There were many university degrees granted posthumously. Those who stayed on the bus lived but before I graduated with my degree, Rakai became a district of ghost towns.[16]"

Until recently, after nearly three decades of research by health organizations worldwide, there were two competing theories about how HIV/AIDS actually started, both of them based on the idea that a virus found in monkeys called Simian Immunodeficiency Virus (SIV) somehow mutated to humans.[17] The first was the "cut hunter" theory where hunters in Zaire, now the Democratic Republic of Congo, ate meat

16  Interview, Phinehas Tukamuhaabwa at his home, January 20, 2005
17  http://www.originofaids.com/

from a diseased monkey, assimilated the disease and began passing it on sexually. The second was the "Polio Inoculation" theory where an experimental anti-polio serum developed in Europe from chimpanzee or macaque substrate was tested on people in the Belgian Congo in the 1950s. The testing actually did occur, but this theory surmises that the virus substrate was taken from diseased animals which allowed it to mutate into humans upon being injected into its test subjects. Conspiracy theorists love this scenario as proof of Western whites wanting to wipe out the African black race, but a vial of the 1950s serum was recently discovered and, after rigorous testing, it was determined that there was no SIV or HIV virus present.

That leaves us with one theory.

In any case, it is widely agreed that the severe poverty conditions with poor sanitation, lack of nutritious food and clean water, working in noxious environments and overwork created a population of people whose physical immunity was extremely debilitated to the point where their bodies allowed the mutation to occur.[18] In Zaire/Congo, such conditions existed in the south and East where massive mining operations had been exploiting workers for decades. In neighboring Uganda, conditions were not much better as the population had struggled with famine, rebellion and a ruined economy almost from the day the nation declared its independence from Great Britain in 1962. Disease was rampant in rural towns such as those in the Rakai district where people struggled to survive day to day. Through the 1960s, 70s and 80s, many countries in Africa were in turmoil causing millions of people to struggle for daily survival which meant tens of millions of people on the continent were in poor health and ripe for disease.

18   http://www.avert.org/historyi.htm

Many factors come into the discussion when talking about how the disease spread worldwide. The first of course is the sex-based exchange of body fluids. In Zaire, formerly the Belgian Congo, Europeans ran the massive mining operations, where the work force was primarily men housed in what can only be described as slave quarters. They worked for pennies. Food was poor. Disease was common. And the opportunity for homosexual liaison was strong. One hunter infected with the newly mutated HIV could easily have introduced infection to a work force of thousands. Then, because government and business operations were driven by Europeans, travel from Africa to Europe was common. When we see AIDS first appeared in Europe and in North America in the homosexual community, it is easy to understand the connection.

But other factors for transmission also existed: rebel armies rife throughout Zaire/Congo from 1960s up to and including today would make sure their conquest of a rival village was complete by raping the women of all ages. The practice, based on ancient tribal customs of conquest, ensured that not only would all the men earn the disease, but so would the victimized women who would pass it along to other innocents or the next army. Other means of transmission included hands with open sores touching the bloody wounds of infected people or ritual circumcision rites for a dozen or so young men all carried out with the same knife.

There is no one scientific theory about how AIDS traveled to Uganda though the country has a long and porous border with Congo. My own theory, pieced together after speaking to people in the area, is that two Congolese fishermen, men who had found a new vocation after years in the mines, took a break from their work one day. They beached their boat on one of the hundreds of Ssese Islands in Lake Victoria. There they were either bitten by monkeys infected with SIV or they ate the meat of diseased animals they had hunted and the disease mutated to become HIV. Heading to the lakeside Rakai District to sell their fish, they no doubt looked forward to celebrating a good day as any man who had money would do. The ladies and the Nile Lager were waiting and Michael rowed the boat ashore. Allelujah.

Every African in every village had heard about or had experienced "bad times" in their history, whether it was famine, rebellion or disease. These were things they could not change. But as a people, they had learned they could usually work hard and wait it out and the family would survive. Yet, well into the 1980s, the disease gained momentum killing, mysteriously enough, only adults. A husband would die of the Slim. His brother would, according to custom, comfort the widow by taking her into his home and into his bed. She would infect him. He would infect his wife. Then he would die. Another brother would step up. The women would die. And the disease spread.

In the cities, prostitution was a common profession for women struggling to feed themselves and their children. Yet, even as people began to die from the disease and its sexual cause was heavily communicated, the number of prostitutes did not decrease. The United Nations pressured the government to make condoms available in "high risk areas," which included bars and wherever Commercial Sex Workers plied their trade. The women soon discovered condoms were good for business in that they learned they could extract a premium price for a client who wanted to go "bareback." Most of the prostitutes and their clients died.

"*SEE?!*" the Pentecostals yelled as they pointed bony fingers at the people. "God brings his wrath on the wicked!!" This was a nice sermon but bad reality because many preachers of all faiths also died of the disease.[19] It was, and to a certain extent, still is common for prosperous middle class men to have "a girl on the side." Young women, often university students short on cash, often sought out "sugar daddies" who provided them with apartments, clothes, cell phones and took them to clubs. In the end, they all died.

At one time, 38% of the Ugandan population was HIV positive. The disease ravaged every neighborhood, every socioeconomic stratum, every job class, and every religion, mostly in people older than 13 years.

It wasn't until 1986 that any government leader in Africa understood what caused the disease. The credit for that discovery goes to Yoweri Kaguta Museveni, the man who wrested the country out of the hands of the last dictator Milton Obote and returned the nation to the people in the form of a British-style parliamentary democracy.

A friend of Ben's arranged for me to meet with His Excellency, the President of Uganda, one Sunday at the State House. Once our van passed through a serpentine path around crash barriers, an iron gate topped with razor wire, past the boyish, dull-eyed sentries fingering ancient rifles and after we left all cameras, cases, telephones and recording devices in the car, we were escorted to an unassuming two-story stucco structure, an office building, set amid manicured lawns and robustly blooming flowers. After a short time in a parlor where we had a delightful conversation with Maggie Kigozi, the nation's Economic Development Manager, we

19    Interview, Frank Isingone at All Saints Church, Kampala, January 7, 2005

were called into the conference room. Waiting there was His Excellency, smiling, apparently glad to greet us. TV cameras rolled. Three nattily dressed ministers of state sat poker-faced at the table with their hands folded. There were a few formalities. Along the way, Ben told His Excellency, known as H.E., that I knew a few words of *Rukiga*, the President's tribal language.

"Tell me," he said. A challenge.

I gave him the full repertoire. *"Mukama asiimwe, owesheimwe.* (Praise the Lord, Brother). *Neb'nyeta Mzee Twesigye,"* I said (They call me the elder who trusts in God) *"Ninduga Chicago America.* (I come from Chicago in America). *Nkaba ndi omusiisi. Hati, Jesu na kanjuna* (I was a sinner but now I walk with Jesus). He listened with a sparkle in his tiny eyes and an amused look on his face. Surely, I had butchered his mother tongue. But when I finished, he clapped his hands with glee. "It is good to hear you speak my language," he announced and burst into a chorus of *tukutendereza*. Then he began to talk about AIDS.

"You know how I discovered we had a problem?" he said. "Fidel Castro told me.

"Only six months after re-establishing the government, I was invited to attend a meeting for the non-aligned African nations in Harare, Zimbabwe. Many countries were trying out Communism then and they wanted to recruit more, so they invited those of us who were not yet Marxist or Leninist or Socialist or Communist to a meeting. I had no intention of becoming a Communist. Idi Amin and Obote were Communists. All the other newly independent states in Africa that tried "African Socialism" were in ruins. But I was curious. Maybe they would build us a road.

"I was there only one day when Castro took me aside. He said, 'Mr. President, I think you have a problem.' I thought: I have more than one problem. The idiot dictators ruined our country. I have no economy, no infrastructure, an incomplete government, an empty treasury, too big an army, refugees everywhere, a starving population... what else could there be? I asked Castro. He said, 'Your predecessor, Obote, sent 80 soldiers to Cuba for military training. We do blood testing of foreign trainees and, of those 80 soldiers, we found 46 to have the Mysterious African Wasting Disease. I thought you would like to know.' I had heard of this disease on the short wave while fighting in the bush. And I knew if the soldiers had it, the population had it. But I didn't know how bad it was. This was, indeed, a problem and I told Castro to send all the soldiers home."

Museveni told how he rushed back to Kampala and called on his Minister of Health and a panel of doctors to determine once and for all what caused the disease. "We need to know," he said them, "Is it the bite of an insect? Is it something in our food or water? Is it people breathing on each other. We need to know." One week later they returned to the President with their findings. Richard Goodgame, an American missionary doctor at Makerere University at the time was on that panel. Now teaching at University of Texas in Galveston, he recalls, "We reported to His Excellency that we had examined every means of disease transmittal. Our conclusion? The disease is spread through the exchange of vital bodily fluids... as in sexual contact and transfusions and the sharing of hypodermic needles and blood rites.

"I remember Museveni sitting back in his chair," Goodgame said. "He relaxed a bit and showed the hint of a smile, the kind you'd see on the face of a man who'd been wrestling with a puzzle for many days and suddenly found the answer. 'This is good news," he declared. "This AIDS is not a medical problem. It is a behavior problem.'"[20]

Within a year, the President mobilized the leadership from all the churches, the schools and the government to impart a single message: Be sexually abstinent until marriage. And be faithful to one person in marriage. That was it. The message poured from loudspeakers in the streets, from pulpits across the land, in newspapers, radios, hand bills, in class rooms at all levels. "Zero Grazing" was the theme. "AIDS Kills" was the message. In other words, to all the truck drivers, prostitutes, horny college students, lusty teenagers waltzing hand in hand into the banana patches, the hookers, men with mistresses and all the sugar daddies, "stop screwing around." It also meant the age-old custom of brothers comforting their siblings' dead widows must stop. Ritual circumcisions must be done with sanitized tools. Wiping the knife on your pants before using it again doesn't count. Those who heeded the message lived. Those who did not died.

The message to young people in schools was and still is: Be abstinent. Do not have sexual relations until you are married. The school evangelists taught: "Just as there are kinds of food you are forbidden to eat as a young person, there is this behavior. You must listen to people who are grown up and know about these things before you partake. Eat the grown up food when you are grown up and not before."

While the President was organizing the nation's voices, Dr. Goodgame working with the Baptist Church issued the first national anti-AIDS campaign called The Answers Program. It was simply a printed flyer that listed the social/medical causes

---

20    Interview, Richard Goodgame via telephone, February 1, 2005

THE CLAY FACTORY OF RAKAI

of the mysterious wasting disease and then offered references from the Bible about leading a non-promiscuous lifestyle. The flyer was handed out with over 15,000 Bibles.

Churches played a vital role in spreading the word as they had people in the far corners of the country and could communicate very quickly. Their message took a spiritual spin: "Love your neighbors but not to death."

Did the President's approach work? He told me, "We used to have STD kiosks all around Kampala. People with a little rash could go get a shot of penicillin. They were very popular. But, within two years of our telling the people they had to change their behavior, the kiosks were all gone. Out of business. No more customers. That was the first sign that our campaign was working."

Museveni's observation – calling the spread of AIDS a behavior problem and not a medical problem - was underscored by the U.S. Surgeon General C.Everett Koop in the first Surgeon General's Report on AIDS dated October, 1986.[21] Within a decade, the new incidence of AIDS dropped from 38% to 5%.

In 2005, I was grazing for artifacts in the craft village in Kampala when I came upon a gracefully shaped pitcher made of red clay. Where does this piece come from, I asked the shopkeeper. "Rakai," she said. I smiled because the district had apparently come back to life.

In 2006, again in the craft village, I found more red clay crockery, this time whimsically formed into the shapes of elephants and hippos. I was holding one of the pieces wondering why it looked so shiny when I was surprised by the shopkeeper coming from behind with "What do you think?"

---

21   http://profiles.nlm.nih.gov/QQ/B/D/R/M/_/qqbdrm.pdf

"From Rakai?" I offered.

"Indeed," she said, smiling her surprise that a *Mzungu* would know such a thing. This was Jane Nabyonga. Far from a mere merchant in National Theatre Craft Village Stall No. 19, Jane told me she had spent time in Peru studying ceramics. Having grown up in the town of Kyotera, she said she knew the clay of Rakai would make good pottery. "Our grandmothers have been making crockery here for hundreds of years," she said. "Moreover, when the indigenous clay was mixed with kaolin mined nearby, it could be formulated to make cookware that was non-toxic, oven-proof and dishwasher safe." Her designs had won awards in Europe.

"Dishwasher safe?" I asked, knowing a Ugandan dishwasher was most likely not a machine but a woman bent over double with a rag and a plastic tub full of water.

"Yes," she said. "For export."

Jane had mobilized women in Rakai to found the Mukisa Mpewo Clay Works in the town of Kyotera. "We have a factory now. You should come see."

We were headed there now.

The land is flat, marshy in places with large patches of dried flood plain and a few scrubby bushes struggling to survive. Young boys waving large Lake Vic tilapia to make them look alive shout at us as we pass... "fresh feesh!" We wonder how fresh. A Jaguar tourist bus approaches and we see three wide-eyed, immobile Tilapians tied to the grille. We take a shortcut at the town of Mbirizi and meander over dusty, washboard roads past lush fields of coffee bushes and banana trees and crossroads villages with dour Muslims staring suspiciously at the van full of white people. We struggle to pass a truck loaded with sacks of dried coffee beans. A herd of goats bolts across the road.

Everything here is tinted with red earth. Cars and trucks raise the dust which settles on the fish, on the roofs, on the bicycles, on the sweat-stained collars. Our tires are muted persimmon. Our car is a magnet and the filings are bits of earth. The creases in our palms are delineated with red earth. It is as though everything that is here is of the earth, moves on the earth and then returns to the earth. Barefooted people spend their days with their skin touching earth. They turn the soil. Its fruit feeds them. Red mud houses offer shelter and protect them from predators. Castoff tires become camouflaged in red dust as the earth works to reclaim them. People die and are buried and return to the dust. It is no ordinary dust. It stains the seams of your shoes. It fills your pores. It stays put in a breeze. When it rains, the water forms the mud into ruts and pits and braids and pools. When it dries, the mud becomes rock. This is the clay of Rakai.

Eventually, we turn onto a paved road where a copse of cellular phone towers in the distance foretells our destination. Soon, the stick-and-mud huts of the open country give way to brick-and-plaster homes with steel doors.

Kyotera town is straight out of the Wild West, a place built alongside the railroad tracks or the river or the harbor, wherever the flow of people would bring commerce. In this case, the traffic flows down main street, a paved thoroughfare for people heading to Tanzania. The settlement is a riot of activity, a nest of ants in alarm, a symphony of survivors in perpetual motion. I don't see one decently built building, but dozens of makeshift huts and lean-tos made of iron sheets. People are everywhere, hammering, bartering and hauling. With a few flat store fronts on main street, all we need is boardwalks and a school marm to complete the picture. The saloon is the "God's Glory Bar." Surely, Wyatt Earp is around here somewhere. A sign welcoming us to town lets us know the Rotary Club meets on Wednesday.

A half hour of wandering amidst the frenzied back streets asking people directions to the clay works brings us to a signless, shuttered building. A man named Antonio asks if he can help. "We are looking for the Clay Works," we say.

"You have found it. I am Jane's neighbor. But everything is done by casual labor these days," he said.

"No factory?" I ask.

"No, but I can show you," he offers. A knock on a nearby door produces a key handed out by an anonymous hand. Antonio opens a door where we see a stall filled with clumpy earth, a pile of greasy kaolin and an old kiln covered in cobwebs. "This is where Jane started," he added. "But no more, Mzee. Today it is casual labor."

I am disappointed because I wanted to take stunning photographs of native people joyously working at bench after bench producing free-trade goods for the world market with their own hands. They are not here, but they must be somewhere. I have seen the end product. It is well made and beautiful. I needed to find out about this casual labor.

"Did you get to Kyotera?" Jane asked when I saw her a few days later.

"I did but all we found was your friendly neighbor Antonio and a dusty old kiln."

"That is where I started," she smiled. "In 17 years, I have learned that we can produce better products if we set up women as home businesses. Casual labor is our factory now. The people actually work harder than if they had to go to a factory building. Their husbands are happier because the women can be at home with the kids. There is no competition with the woman at the next bench. I can hire as many people as want to work. So I have people in Kyotera, in Kampala, and several places in between. It took a long time to get here, but it works. The Clay Works."

I saw in Jane's face the spirit of recovering Uganda. People working hard to pull themselves out of Dictator-imposed and UN-fueled wilderness, people using the resources beneath their feet to create meaningful jobs and a sense of prosperity. This woman had an idea which, with hard work and trial-and-error, turned into a product that involved the management and coordination of many hands and created an income potential that equals PhD or professional wages in this country.[22] Today the fruit of those hands feeds whole families. Jane provided a spark, an idea that has become magnified, touching more and more lives every day. She did it herself. Without the World Bank or the UN or micro-loans. The Rakai District is alive again and it is only thanks to the hard work and ingenuity of Jane and ten thousand others with the same sense of survival. It is their example that will teach young people to dream and dream big, to believe anything is possible even in the face of national tragedy.

---

22   http://www.blackwell-synergy.com/doi/abs/10.1111/1468-5949.00295

# Condom Wars

*"When elephants fight, only the grass suffers."*
-African proverb

When His Excellency President Museveni declared the AIDS crisis in his country a behavior problem in 1986, he had no idea he was poking a stick into a very large hive of bees.

It took some years for the magnitude of the epidemic to become known to world's public health institutions and for them to decide upon a workable solution to slowing the spread of the disease. The institutions – the World Health Organization, the United Nations (ultimately UN-AIDS and The Global Fund), the Center for Disease Control in the U.S. – and others – were challenged to come up with a single, easy-to-sell solution that would work worldwide. The Uganda President's pragmatic solution – tell the people what causes the disease, tell them to abstain from sexual relations before marriage, tell them to be faithful exclusively to their spouse or partner – was simply dismissed as unworkable by Western aid institutions. They sought a solution that was based not on abstract ideals but on something tangible. Their solution was the condom, a device that had been available in Uganda since at least 1980.

From the public health point of view, the condom was a uni-laterally simple, practical way to fight AIDS. But getting the population to actually use it was not easy and so the field of social engineering was born to sell the concept to third world people. This approach conflicted directly with what became the social vaccine of behavior change.

The clash between the two points of view – behavior change vs. prophylaxis - became known as The Condom Wars, a conflict that has changed shape in venues throughout Africa and the rest of the world but remains a clash of wills wherever it goes.

The participants in The Condom Wars include condom manufacturers, governments in the East, West and South, inter-national public health organizations, various national leaders, social researchers, the ecclesiastical community, non-denom-inational faith-based organizations, independent "watchdog" organizations, the gay rights community and the medical com-munity. As in any war, there are many people crossing into each other's territory to make sorties against the enemy.

One notable skirmish occurred at the UN-sponsored International AIDS Conference in Bangkok, Thailand in 2004. When President Museveni was introduced at the open-ing ceremony, he attracted thunderous applause as the leader of the one African nation that has beaten back the epidemic. He shared the dais with UN Secretary General Kofi Annan, Thai Prime Minister Thaksin Shinawatra, film star Richard Gere and Miss Universe 2004 Jennifer Hawkins. The next day he was a featured speaker and, as usual, he stressed that changing behavior and not the distribution of condoms was the key to his country's well-documented success. Once again, he stressed that condoms have a role to play but they are not the panacea solution. He reiterated that Uganda had the lowest condom usage in Africa and the best record in reducing the disease.[23] A large contingent of gay rights activists tried to shout him down, but Museveni shouted right back.

The following day, the Wall Street Journal published this editorial:

*"Abstain from sex or delay having sex if you are young and not married, Be faithful to your sexual partner (zero-grazing), after testing, or use a Condom properly and consistently if you are going to move around. This has now been globally popularized as the ABC strategy".*

— Ugandan President Yoweri Museveni, in an address Monday to the International AIDS Conference in Bangkok.

You would think that the common-sense message above would be embraced by all reasonable people, especially those whose avowed interest it is to staunch the spread of HIV/AIDS. But these words, and many others like it, have landed Mr. Museveni in a controversy with the hyper-politicized activists who attend these conferences.

This, you see, is because merely to suggest a solution to HIV infection that does not put condoms as the first and only line of defense is to do several bad things. One is to put oneself on the same side as the abstinence-counseling Vatican and U.S. President George W. Bush, rated as bad guys by audiences such as this. The good guys, the United Nations, the

---

23    New Vision report by Charles Wendo and John Odyek, July 13, 2004 http://www.aegis.com/news/nv/2004/nv040721.html

World Health Organization and the various NGOs, all support condoms.

To advise self-control even as part of the solution is, moreover, to imply that individual decisions about sex and drug use are partly responsible for the spread of HIV/AIDS, and this is a connection that activists have resisted from the start of this plague. Sometimes it seems that their interest is not solely or even primarily in stopping AIDS. Rather, it seems to be in gaining social acceptance for promiscuity, which is why condom use must now be taught in schools.

The activists' hijacking of these conferences, unfortunately, has made them at best expensive talkfests, at worst an impediment to finding real solutions. At the U.N.-sponsored conference in Bangkok this week, proponents of condoms have vastly outnumbered those who dare support abstinence, just as those who demonize pharmaceutical companies for patenting drugs that combat HIV have overwhelmed those with the temerity to suggest that only the profit motive guarantees a cure one day.

In Mr. Museveni, however, the activists have met a formidable foe who has become a gadfly on this issue. They are confounded by the fact that, unlike the mostly Western, middle-class activists, Mr. Museveni is actually an African leader successfully battling the disease. He will go any place that will have him and repeat his home truths.

The first truth is that condoms have a failure rate, however minimal. Even the pro-condom WHO only claims that "consistent and correct" condom use only

reduces infection by 90%. The second is that condoms institutionalize promiscuity, the behavior that
is at the heart of the sexually transmitted epidemic.

So while the activists insist on condoms for fur-
tive but supposedly non-infectious sexual trysts, the
Ugandan speaks of love and commitment. And as is
often the case, form accompanies substance. While
the activists alternate between angry and infantile
behavior, chanting and waving blood-stained signs,
or dressing up like giant condoms, the African simply spreads his message with words of reason, statistics and dignity.

The best way to fight AIDS, he told an audience
that grew more stunned by the minute, was with
"relationships based on love and trust, instead of
institutionalized mistrust, which is what the condom
is all about." Condoms, he said, "are not the ulti-
mate solution to this problem." A condom-focused
campaign, he added for good measure, would only
prevent societies from doing something about the
root causes of the disease. "AIDS is mainly a moral,
social and economic problem," he said. To rub salt in
the wound, he praised President Bush for commit-
ting billions to fight AIDS in Africa.

The activists were not amused by this message.
"It seems slightly drawn by ideology rather than an
assessment of needs on the ground," observed Mabel
van Oranje, a director for financier George Soros's
Open Society Institute in Holland. Leading the charge
against the Bush administration was the Democratic
Party's congresswoman Barbara Lee, who said that

"an abstinence-until-marriage program is not only irresponsible, it's really inhumane."

Both women argued that Mr. Museveni's approach could not be tried in Africa because women's first sexual experience is "involuntary." This is one of those arguments that at first sounds plausibly substantive, until it dawns on you that not many rapists really do bother to use condoms.

For his part Tim Brown of the East West Center in Hawaii told the Associated Press, "I disagree with (Mr. Museveni). Condoms are greatly shortchanged in Africa as a prevention method." Mr. Brown made the following claim: "If you increase condom use by 50%, I guarantee you that HIV will go down by 50%."

It's easy to "guarantee" these things, of course. Less easy is what Mr. Museveni has done with Uganda. While the rest of sub-Saharan Africa is ever more mired in AIDS, his country has gone from a 30% infection rate in the early 1990s to 6% today, a success rate the president attributes to abstinence.[24]

Interestingly enough, teaching people to use condoms requires changing behavior, something the anti-abstinence people argue cannot be done. One of my favorite stories told to me by a Roman Catholic leader, involves a team of "condom trainers," mobile health workers traveling on motorcycles, sent to an outlying village to teach people how to use the prophylactic devices in order to not only protect themselves from AIDS but also to prevent unwanted pregnancy. When news of the training was announced in the village, many women

---

24    *Wall Street Journal,* Review & Outlook, "Museveni's ABCs" July 14, 2004 http://www.ph.ucla.edu/epi/seaids/musevenisABCs.html

became excited, primarily about the possibility of preventing pregnancies.

Standing in front of the village, the trainers used bananas to illustrate the proper way to apply a condom, all the while extolling the virtues of latex and its ability to protect both the wearer and his partner. They told the people if they used these devices, they would not die from AIDS and they would have fewer babies. After demonstrating the technique, the villagers were encouraged to practice on bananas as well. The training ended, a large box of condoms was left behind and the trainers went on to the next village.

Six months later the trainers stopped by for a follow-up visit. The chief received them with typically warm Ugandan hospitality, but when they asked, "How's it going," the chief shook his head. Sadly, he said, the condoms do not seem to be working. We still have women becoming pregnant and people are still getting sick. "We are doing everything you taught us but it is not working," he said. On further investigation, the team found the chief had spoken the truth. Every home had a banana wearing a condom. The villagers somehow never realized the device was meant to be worn by a human being.

From a weak start in the 1980s and well into the 21st century, the world's public health advocates pushed condoms on Africa, 20 million of them annually in Uganda alone by the year 2000. Western health organizations sent highly paid consultants called social engineers throughout Africa to advise governments on how to condomize their populations. The doors were opened to private condom manufacturers who staged elaborate marketing campaigns including billboards, handbills and radio advertising that proclaimed the benefits of condoms for all to see. "Yes," Ben laments. "This public marketing in effect told people the moral behavior change was now unnecessary... here is an easier way. But it was, and is, a lie."

The condom marketing machine reached a new peak in 2005 with the introduction of the "Three Amigos" in South Africa. "Let's make the condom lovable," said Brent Quinn, a 45 year-old South African screenwriter. He was talking about his idea of a cartoon series featuring three talking prophylactics called Shaft, Dick and Stretch that appeared for months, often twenty times a day, in a series of animated public service announcements on the South African Broadcasting Corporation. Quinn and his business partner, Canadian television producer Firdaus Kharas had just finished a round of meetings in Washington and New York with UNICEF, the U.S. State Department, the World Health Organization and the World Bank as they sought funding for worldwide distribution of the new media project they claimed had become a cult sensation in South Africa.

The three amigos go on adventures, Quinn explained, three mates out to get lucky. One soccer-themed spot says, "You just can't score without a condom." Quinn says they are a hit with young children, including his own, aged seven and nine.

The spots were delivered on DVDs which included a message from South African Archbishop Desmond Tutu who is quoted in the program's promotional material as saying, "Young people do not respond well on being told what to do even when such instruction is in their own self interest. Animated characters are a non-threatening, non-authoritarian vehicle for communication." It is reported that the Nobel laureate read the scripts for the spots and immediately lent his support.

Quinn reported a warm reception from organizations approached in North America. "Except for the U.S. State Department," he said. "Their priority is more A and B... abstinence and being faithful." Quinn considered adding an episode about abstinence. "Cartoon condoms talking about abstinence," he said. "How funny is that?"[25]  The Republic of Uganda respectfully and immediately denied visas to The Three Amigos when it heard of their plan for worldwide distribution.

Often, too often, aid money was tied to condom usage. Governments could get food aid but only if they bought condoms. Governments could get funding for major public infrastructure, but only if they bought condoms. In study after study commissioned by the West, condoms were shown to be the most effective means for stopping the disease. And soon, the Uganda program that began as AB became ABC, meaning be abstinent, be faithful, but if you cannot do those things, use a condom.

President Museveni told me, "A and B were working for us but if C would save even more lives in our country, then who am I to object? I am open to anything that will eradicate this disease." Then he said, "What irritates me is when people who are not from this country or who do not know our culture try to force their solutions on us using badly needed aid for other things as an enticement. I have told them many times to take their handouts and go home." [26]

One example was the US-based Planned Parenthood (PPH) that staged National Condom Week beginning on

25  "Canadian Promotes Cartoon Condoms Against AIDS" by Evelyn Leopold, Reuters on-line, January 11, 2005
26  "Spread Condoms, Not AIDS," Planned Parenthood Press Release, February 14, 2003

February 14, 2004 coinciding with Valentine's Day to encourage activists to send condoms to Africa along with a message to President George W. Bush. The campaign promised activists that if they sent the White House a message requesting greater condom availability and condom information to Africa, PPH would send a condom to Africa on the President's behalf. Upon hearing about this campaign, President Museveni sent a note to Gloria Feldt, President of Planned Parenthood Federation of America, emphatically requesting that her organization should NOT send ANY condoms to Uganda. Museveni was then accused by PPH as being anti-condom. Ms. Feldt resigned from PPH in 2005 but her successor continues to rail against abstinence-only programs to this day.

Interestingly enough, PPH is not only an advocacy organization, but they are also a major manufacturer and distributor of condoms which come in a variety of colors and flavors. Their activist organization's statistics claim more than 1.1 billion condoms are needed in sub-Saharan Africa for HIV/AIDS prevention efforts. This also seems to be good news for the manufacturing side of the organization.

As we saw with Mr. Museveni on Valentine's Day, rejection of such aid was often regarded as an "anti-condom" attitude which fueled the publicity machines of Planned Parenthood and other condomizers to turn out a decade's worth of sharply accusing sound-bites. One article entitled "Condom Wars" attempts to paint African leaders such as Museveni as backward, ungrateful and uncaring about the welfare of their people. Pro and anti-condom groups launched media-based broadsides at each other. Uganda's First Lady Janet Museveni remains a passionate advocate and cheerleader for abstinence and is often portrayed as the poster person for anti-condom sentiment. We have already described how large contingents of protesters, mostly homosexual, regularly boo President Museveni as he proclaims on the world's stage that A and B are preferable to C in fighting the spread of AIDS. And meanwhile, the disease spreads, most prevalently in South Africa and Nigeria where condom sales are booming, people die and growing numbers of orphans gather in clumps to stare hopelessly into the future.

In places where the Uganda government was persuaded to bring condoms into its population, it restricted the free distribution to "high risk" areas – bars and night clubs where prostitution was prevalent and on university campuses.

Churches resisted advocating condoms for years, but eventually the Anglican-based Church of Uganda began to adopt President Museveni's opinion – if a condom will help save one more life, it is worth it. Leadership emphasized that condoms are not a substitute for careful behavior – abstinence and being faithful – and warned people that a condom is not a license to be sexually active. They regularly cited evidence that condoms are not reliable and that there is much to understand before using one. Here are some of their sources and arguments (the italics where they appear are mine):

- The International Standards Organization considers an acceptable breakage rate for plastic condoms at 5%. "Imagine," one clergyman said, "If you were to fly from the USA to Europe and five out of every 100 flights crashed into the sea. Such performance would not be acceptable. People would not fly to Europe." Julian Edwards, Director General of Consumers International said, "If a breakage rate of 5% became the norm, more than a million extra exposures to AIDS would occur every day."[27]

- Consumer Reports tested 23 brands of latex condoms of which two were shown to have a greater tendency to fail. *How many Ugandans read Consumer Reports?*

- Size matters. If a man wears a condom that is too large it can easily slip off during intercourse and cause infection beyond transmitted disease.

- Condoms should be stored in a cool, dry place. *If you live on the equator and carry a condom in your pocket, does that count?*

- Follow package directions. *It is night, the beer and the dancing have worked their magic and the girl is ready. Excuse me, honey, I need to read this package.*

- Use only water-based lubricants such as Astorglide or K-Y jelly. Oil-based lubricants such as petroleum jelly, baby oil or body lotion can weaken the latex.

- Condoms may be made of latex, synthetic material or lambskin. There are pros and cons of each.[28]

- Planned Parenthood advises: "If a condom breaks during intercourse, you should take steps to protect yourself and your partner from a possible unintended pregnancy or sexually transmitted infection, including HIV. Emergency contraception should be considered as well as testing for STIs and HIV."[29] *Keep that fire extinguisher handy.*

---

27   "Warning on Condom Safety," BBC News July 17, 2002. http://news.bbc. co.uk./1/hi/health/2100972.stm

28   "Condoms – Extra Protection," *Consumer Reports*, February 2005. www.consumerreports.org

29   "Planned Parenthood Condoms are Safe," by Peter Durkin, *Lufkin Daily News*, January 12, 2005. www.lufkindailynews.com

In 2002, bowing to UN pressure, the government of Uganda issued a contract to purchase 80 million Engabu brand condoms manufactured by the Guangzhou Rubber Factory No. 7 in China. Having paid $2 million for the order, condoms soon began to arrive in batches of 10 million. They were intended for free distribution to the population. In one batch, after arriving at the government's National Medical Stores facility and then distributed in March of 2003, some condoms were suspected to be defective after the public complained about a bad smell. [30]

"Yes," said Bank of Uganda Governor Mutebile who paid the bill, "I'm told the entire container reeked when it came into the warehouse. We distributed the condoms and then recalled them but I don't think we got them all because they were still using them in the prisons (for conjugal visits) for a long time. They tell us to store these things in a cool, dry place. But they were shipped in un-refrigerated metal containers and of course the transport route from China to Mombasa is tropical. The real problem it turned out was contaminated lubricant packed with the condoms. The net effect was the sour solution weakened the latex and many of the condoms fell apart. We never did get a credit for that shipment."

"After the Engabu problem, we changed the procedure for importing condoms in the country," said Dr. Elizabeth Madraa, the Ministry of Health's National AIDS Programme Manager. "We now inspect them before they are shipped and when they arrive, but for awhile, we had to intercept other shipments and make sure they were OK. This lengthened the process of distributing them which triggered a shortage since many Ugandans had become frequent users, believing

---

30   "More Engabu Condoms Coming," by John Odyek, New Vision on-line, January 6, 2005. http://allafrica.com/stories/printable/200501060528.html

that they were protecting themselves against AIDS if they did. Ugandans used between 80 and 100 million condoms annually as part of the country's anti-AIDS strategy."[31]

Condom Wars that started as a battle between West and South evolved into a worldwide battle between the Religious Right and World Public Health, a battle with fewer skirmishes today, but one that is kept alive by James Dobson and writers for Christian magazines and websites. Reporting on a new round of tests of condoms by Consumer Reports, Jane Jiminez writing for Agape Press of the Christian News Service wrote:

"In a well-lit laboratory, one by one, a laboratory tech unwraps each condom and follows a well-rehearsed, methodical, and uniform procedure to place the condom on sterile lab equipment and inflate it with air until it bursts. No STDs are present. No sperm, no emotions, no shadows and no youthful inexperience will cloud the results.

"Using the context of controlled laboratory perfection, some educators want us to believe we can rest assured that condoms will save our children from the consequences of sex. Touting statistics from laboratory tests, they say condoms *only fail three percent of the time.*

"In the context of real life, measuring the failure of condoms in the shadows, in the heat of the moment, the statistics demonstrate time and again that context counts. Condoms fail to prevent pregnancy 13-15% of the time for real people outside of laboratories. If the real people are teenagers, the failure rate can be as high as 22%."[32]

Church leaders in Uganda reluctantly acknowledge a prophylactic device might be necessary in some cases, such as

---

31   "New Condom Quality Control Rules Cause Shortage in Uganda," *Health News Designerz*, December 14, 2004. www.health.news.designerz.com

32   "Condoms: Context Counts," by Jane Jimenez, *Agape Press*, Christian News Service, January 11, 2005

for married couples where one of the partners is HIV+ or in high-risk areas such as prisons, nightclubs or refugee camps where the church has little influence. The last holdout was the Roman Catholic Church whose policy against any type of birth control remains in force worldwide. Yet, even here, concern for protecting the health of parishioners eventually overcame birth control policy and now the Roman Catholic hierarchy allows but does not encourage an ABC policy in Uganda.

The more churches wrestled with the issue of condoms, the more they stepped up the education of their flocks on A and B. The government wages a ceaseless information campaign, especially in schools where signs such as "Stay Pure" "No Sex before Marriage," "AIDS Kills," "Stay Virgin" can be found tacked to trees or stenciled on walls. Government health clinics nationwide offer AIDS counseling as a standard part of their service.

Shortly after the turn of the 21st century, when it seemed the condom wars would never end, the AB message received an enormous boost with the onset of the President Bush's Emergency Plan for AIDS Relief (PEPFAR), based entirely on what is known as "The Uganda Model" for stopping the spread of the virus.

The idea for PEPFAR was introduced in 2003 largely as the result of research undertaken for USAID by Harvard University's Edward C. (Ted) Green, Dr. Rand Stoneburner and Dr. Norman Hearst. In a presentation before the Medical Institute for Sexual Health in Austin, TX to Ambassador Randall Tobias, the Global AIDS Coordinator and approximately 35 appointees of the Bush Administration from the White House and the Department of Health and Human Services, Green stated that worldwide, 8,000 people die of AIDS every day, the equivalent of 20 fully-loaded Boeing 747s crashing, killing everyone on board, day after day, year after year. He told how, at the urging of USAID, more than 100 developing countries had completed the formulation of strategic AIDS plans by December, 2002.

Heralded as one of the most objective presentations on dealing with the AIDS pandemic, participants dealt only with statistical fact, openly avoiding issues such as "Is my personal or corporate ideology or time-honored presupposition threatened? Is my personal or corporate prestige threatened? Is my person or corporate financial future threatened? Was a program developed by me or my group of our friends?" The purpose of the presentation was to answer the question: "Is there one place in the world, shown by scientific study, to have reversed a generalized HIV epidemic for an extended number of years?" The answer was yes. Uganda. As Rand Stoneburner stated: "Uganda is the only country in the world where HIV prevalence in a heterosexual population has undergone such a dramatic and sustained decline (a decrease of HIV prevalence in pregnant women from 30% to less than 6% 1990-2000)

Norman Hearst, Professor of Epidemiology and Biostatistics at the University of California, San Francisco School of Medicine reported: "There is no known example of a country that has turned back a generalized heterosexual epidemic of HIV primary through condom promotion. Contrary to popular belief, there is little evidence to show that all this condom promotion we've been doing all these years in African countries with generalized epidemics has made any difference.

"Fortunately for Uganda," he added, "There weren't a lot of foreign experts telling them how to do things in the late 1980s and early 1990s so they did things their own way. That's when

Museveni was going around with his bullhorn telling people about Zero Grazing and, in the circles I travel (the so-called AIDS experts), everybody thought he was a clown, a buffoon. Everybody made fun of him. Well, it turns out he was exactly right and we were all wrong."[33]

Soon after this conference, President Bush launched PEPFAR as a $15 billion fund to support an abstinence-first education effort in seven African nations. The program was ultimately expanded to include many Caribbean countries. Deemed successful by USAID, the President proposed doubling the size of the program in 2007.

PEPFAR infuriated the UN-based health community as it emphasized abstinence over condoms. In 2005, Dr. Ruben DelPrado, the Uganda coordinator for UNAIDS was asked to leave the country because of his vociferous objection to a public health policy that reduces an emphasis on condoms and also for lobbying for homosexual rights in a nation where homosexuality is illegal. Speaking from his office in Geneva after leaving the country, Dr. DelPrado told me, "That government is making a huge mistake. There's no way an ideology can be used to fight an epidemic."

"By ideology, you mean marriage?" I asked.

"Yes. Marriage. Being faithful. It is against human nature. You cannot stop promiscuity in that culture. The only way to fight the spread of AIDS there is to provide condoms."[34]

In fact, some studies conclude that condoms are being used and are apparently being a barrier to the spread of AIDS. The UK-based International Community of Women Living with HIV/AIDS is an organization that claims to be

33   http:\\www.pacha.gov/meetings/presentations/po304, Presentation January 8, 2004
34   Interview, Dr. Reuben DelPrado interview, via telephone, February 10, 2005

an international network that strives to share with the global community the experiences, views and contributions of 19 million HIV+ women worldwide. In an effort to bring a voice of reason among the condom warriors, they published a position paper subtitled "The war against condoms in Uganda is misguided and inappropriate and unfortunate in the fight against HIV/AIDS and it should end."

In the paper they speak of a highly promiscuous society – "In a 13-year study (1990-2002) followup study on HIV incidence and prevalence in rural Southwest Uganda where sex is believed to be elaborate, a significant reduction in prevalence and incidence was revealed but there was no reported reduction of multiple regular partners, no reduction in the number of casual partners, there was a consistent increase in condom use in HIV-negatives, young people 13-34 years old."

Also: "In a local quality assurance sampling survey report carried out in 19 districts in Uganda on knowledge among young people on ABC as a strategy of HIV prevention, it was indicated that the youth have more knowledge on condom use (74.8%) than on either abstinence (52.3%) or being faithful (28.2%). It was also found that condom use among young people with non-regular partners was high (55.7%).

And finally: In spite of our campaigns, many young Ugandans, even those in schools, live active sex lives. Others, especially girls are subjected to premarital sex by older men. Many girls and women, especially in war and conflict areas are forced or enticed into sex with no choice or power to abstain or be faithful. The high rates of teenage pregnancies say it all."

In direct response to the church's effort to minimize reliance on condoms, they conclude: "By declaring war on distribution of condoms among youth disposes many Ugandans to risk of infection."[35]

I find this point of view a little naïve, thinking that soldiers raiding villages, rapists or even predatory "sugar daddies" would even consider using condoms. "Excuse me, Miss. I'm part of a rebel group marauding your village and we're gang-raping all the women. Give me just a moment while I put on this Pleasure Seeker condom. Don't worry. I'm using a new, clean one between victims."

Perhaps the most authoritative voice on the subject comes from Ted Green himself, a research scientist at Harvard University and author of *Rethinking AIDS Prevention*. The title of the book is really a research-driven shift in the author's point of view from condom-pusher to abstinence-believer. We've already mentioned Green's research was the basis for PEP-FAR in 2004, but in 2003, the US Agency for International Development (USAID) asked the sociologist to study the long-term benefits achieved through the various AIDS prevention methods in Africa. The researcher says when his report was submitted, USAID shelved it and hired a condom advocate to conduct a further study which it ultimately accepted. Green's study had concluded the "ABC method – abstinence, being faithful in marriage and Condoms only for high –risk populations – was most effective in the dramatic reduction of AIDS cases in Uganda.

"We have in our possession a social vaccine," Green said, referring to a point made by fellow AIDS researcher Rand Stoneburner. "The biomedical vaccines we talk about for AIDS have been 10 years away for 20 years. They're still far

---

35   "Position Statement on Condoms vs. Abstinence as HIV/AIDS Prevention Strategies in Uganda" International Community of Women Living with AIDS (ICW) developed by a Civil Society Coalition for HIV/AIDS Prevention, July 2004

away and no one is expecting such a vaccine to be more than about 35 to 40 percent effective when and if we get one. In fact, a new, more aggressive strain of the AIDS virus has just recently emerged, setting pharmaceutical solutions back another decade. But, as Stoneburner has been saying, we already have a social vaccine promoting partner reductions, fidelity, monogamy and abstinence."

Green first focused on the facts in Uganda in 1993 when he was a social engineer and self-avowed condom advocate. He says he was stunned to see infection rates were falling because of something other than condoms. "Nobody believed that the rates were coming down and nobody believed that it had anything to do with abstinence and faithfulness," he said. "I told USAID in a report that's published in my book 'Ah! Look, they're doing something different and it is working. My recommendation was to put more resources into abstinence and faithfulness.' Those recommendations were ignored."

Green cited a parallel situation: "You would advise young people not to start smoking and say to others: If you already smoke, consider giving it up or at least have fewer cigarettes per day," he said. "But for the last 20 plus years we have not been able to say that about sexual behavior. We haven't said straight out: 'If you're young, don't start until you're married and, if you've already started, stick to one partner. Don't have dozens or scores or hundreds of partners.' In any infectious disease, you want to limit your number of contacts. How do you limit your contacts when it comes to something that's sexually transmitted except with fidelity and abstinence?

"There is a trend in Africa toward abstinence and fidelity despite lack of funding for that sort of promotion," Green said. "Faith-based organizations have been the major voices for abstinence in Uganda, but they have been sidelined. Almost none of them have been funded by major donors, or major organizations that fund AIDS programs. We found that if you ask people in those countries why they're choosing those methods, it's typically because some religious group told them they have to do it or they'll die. Such blatant truth-telling is stemming the tide of the AIDS epidemic in some African nations. Clearly, here, making the moral argument works."

Rev. Martin Ssempa, an outspoken abstinence advocate at Makerere Community Church, echoes the findings of Harvard researcher Green. "Ted demonstrates how religious conviction can impact science. In Uganda, faith as expressed by A & B has an impact on the public health. But there are influential people here, even in the church, who refuse to downplay the role of condoms. One of them is Gideon Byamugisha, an HIV+ Anglican priest who is seemingly an enemy of ABC. He uses his collar and his status to push condoms. I have had to battle him. He uses his victim status and that is hard to challenge. He came in about 1994 as a voice for ABC, but he really saying the condom was responsible for the lower incidence of the disease. He goes on with a new kind of hogwash. His was a voice that encouraged the expert community to finally say ABC brought down the incidence of AIDS, but when I hear them I get angry. He is one of those who are redefining the theme, a new breed of AIDS experts both local and international, not philosophically opposed to ABC but treating A&B as a joke. They laugh at it. Essentially, they are saying the condom did it. As a pastor, I think ABC is simple concept. But Gideon makes us more confused."[36]

---

36   Interview, Martin Ssempa, Makerere Community Church, January 15, 2005

The on-line fact sheet on condoms by the U.S. Centers for Disease Control and Prevention at www.cdc.gov used to begin with this statement: "Condoms are effective in preventing HIV and other STDs." The fact sheet was removed from the website in 2002 and was later replaced with one that states: "The surest way to avoid transmission of sexually transmitted diseases is to abstain from sexual intercourse or be in a long-term monogamous relationship with someone whom you know is not infected."[37]

Now, more than 20 years into the battle, the various parties involved in the Uganda condom wars seem to have reached détente. The nation imports and distributes more than 100 million condoms per year for free distribution. Abstinence was and still is the main message painted on scrap lumber signs tacked to trees and buildings at public schools nationwide. The government continues its 1986 message of "Zero Grazing" at public health clinics nationwide. Churches throughout the land speak openly of abstinence and being faithful. Billboards throughout Kampala, once filled with condom advertising and later a well-crafted, PEPFAR-funded abstinence message, now present the benefits of cellular telephone service.

But somehow this device, this tiny bit of latex touches one's morality, religious beliefs, opinions on sexual persuasion and concern for humanity. It incites the social extremists to rhetoric and vitriol. It pits would-be colonizers against those fiercely defending their independence. A powerful thing indeed.

Meanwhile, in Uganda, the government and the people forge ahead knowing what works for them. Before there was a

---

37   "Condoms – Extra Protection," *Consumer Reports*, February 2005. www.consumerreports.org

UN program, before any leader of any country acknowledged the AIDS problem, before anti-retrovirals, and before AIDS was dubbed in the West as "the gay disease," Uganda identified the problem and found a solution that fit their culture. Today, the rate of AIDS infection holds steady at 6%. Young people are delaying the age of first sexual encounter, now at 17 years. The number of men having multiple partners has dropped. Abstinence and being faithful – zero grazing – worked then and continues to work today.

# The Power of Abstinence

*"Virginity is Cool"*
- Martin Ssempa

It is Saturday night on Munongo Road in the heart of Kampala and there is sex in the syrupy equatorial air. Young men and women, feeling good, are hanging out. The girls, poetry in tight jeans and tube tops, their hair just right, with pouty looks, knowing smiles and eyes that say "available" greet the boys, strutting in their best shirts, smelling good with shillings in their pockets and only too willing to oblige. They sway to the throbbing music from a dozen loud speakers. Billboards promise popularity and success with a Nile Lager. Open-air bars and discos filled with people ripple with too-loud laughter. A tender touch, a whispered word, a slow dance and the night is young. Western rap echoes tribal drums that touch the ancient souls of the young, and for this generation, the effect is the same as it was for their ancestors. Undulating hips, the heat of the night, a Waragi for the lady, a moist sheen on the skin, the throb of a drum, a taste just to feel good, and the evening wouldn't be complete without...

Two miles away, the roar of a crowd swells over Makerere University. Some 1,200 students fill the bleachers at the swimming complex to sing, laugh, shout and pray with Pastor Martin Ssempa, who has only one message: sex is a precious gift from God. Ssempa, an evangelical pastor and social activist talks about family – the goal of life, often including his wife Tracey and their children on stage.

He invites visiting missionaries and colleagues to talk about their families and their walks with God. "If you want to live a long life pleasing to you and pleasing to God," he says softly into the microphone, "You will keep this gift, this treasure of self, hidden away until you present it to your lover on your wedding night."

He speaks to the crowd as if each person were sitting with him privately in a little office. "Isn't it interesting," he says, "that Satan, the tempter and destroyer, would show up with death right at that place where we are meant to create and cherish life? You can choose life or you can choose death. God wants you to choose life. Go ahead. Choose life."

The people he is reaching at this university of 40,000 students are enthusiastic and inspired. One young man has formed a hip-hop band called "No Hell" to take the abstinence message to the streets of Kampala with original rap. Another young lady has formed a group of dormitory-based abstinence clubs. Another forms Virginity Rallyes that demonstrate all around Kampala.

And now, after years of delivering the message, Ssempa looks into the growing number of faces at his overflow Saturday night rallies and says simply, "Yeah. Virginity is cool."

I wondered, thinking back to my own college days, how many students at a Big Ten university would take time on a Saturday night to attend an abstinence rally. The thought process would go something like: "Beer, abstinence, beer, abstinence. Beer." If there was a meeting, it would most likely be clandestine, a cabal of the deliberately chaste, held in a hidden corner at an out-of-the-way place off campus, not at the University swimming auditorium. But here, tonight, at a meeting called Prime Time, were over a thousand young people with not only the ubiquitous access to beer but also with free condoms and the temptations of Mulongo Road, all listening, rapt, absorbing this message of abstinence.

"You know," Pastor Ssempa told me earlier that day, "When students were dying from the disease – when their friends could see them wasting away – there was fear. It was easy for people to understand the message of abstinence and being faithful then. I myself watched a cousin's sister die in Masaka in 1986. The *New Vision* newspaper had a column called "The Weekly Topic" where they reported 50 died in Rakai this month, then it was 80 dying in Rakai the next month and so on for years. There was a famous rock singer named Philly Lutaaya who got AIDS and then started to sing about what a tragedy it was for young people. He sang until he died and was a huge influence on a generation. Myself, I wasn't a Christian at the time and was living the life, actually had a baby, and realized if I kept going, I could die. We were all scared and I remember being an undergraduate at Makerere University when your friend Ben came through and presented a skit on AIDS. I was personally saved by Ben during a fellowship meeting afterward and I'm sure that is why I am alive today. That's how I know we can have influence over these kids. I was one of them. The threat was clear then. Today, it's not so easy."

We had met over a meal of chicken pancakes at The Crocodile Restaurant in Kampala, a Western style eatery run by a blonde, sixtyish Belgian woman who directed her staff gently and with infinite patience, reminding me of Meryl Streep quietly managing the plantation workers in *Out of Africa*.

"What do you mean," I asked. "Aren't students still getting AIDS?"

"Oh, yes. They still get it," he replied. "And I fear they are getting it in far greater frequency than they were ten years ago. Remember my telling you about Philly Lutaaya? He had his message. Tonight there is a popular rock group performing on campus with the message: 'Slim-U is Dead.' Slim, of course, was what people called the disease before it was called HIV/AIDS. The problem is that HIV+ people look normal today. Anti-retroviral drugs, the ARVs now in plentiful supply mask the disease. You don't see people walking around on campus with big purple sores. The university hospital is no longer full of people wasting away. People live longer so we don't graduate dead students with posthumous degrees much anymore. If you talk to these kids, they will tell you it is okay to party once again."[38]

"So," I asked. "The ARVs make people less sick and help them live longer, almost normal lives. What's wrong with that?"

"It is a blessing for those people," the pastor said. "But the reality is, they still have the disease. They can still pass it on. Because they look normal and feel normal, they are less inclined to take precautions – to abstain or use condoms – or even tell their sexual partners they are HIV positive. The

---

38   Interview with Martin Ssempa, Kampala, January 15, 2004

partners certainly have no way of telling. And here's the real irony of it all: because these people can live five or ten or more years beyond where they would have probably died without the ARVs, they have the potential of infecting many, many more people."

I paused to think about what the pastor just told me. Over the last decade, there had been enormous pressure put upon health researchers and pharmaceutical companies to develop and anti-AIDS vaccine. Billions of dollars had been spent to find "the silver bullet." No cure has been found but a stop-gap vaccine had been developed – the Anti Retroviral - that would diminish the damage the HIV virus would have on one's immune system. Once ARVs emerged, the world's public health community demanded the vaccine should be made available at very low cost. The pharmaceutical companies objected – how could they recoup their massive research costs? There were tariff issues and importing issues and infrastructure issues. There was loud public debate for awhile between the spokes-people for the world's sick and helpless and the profit-hungry corporate giants with a few Hollywood celebrities chiming in with their utterly uninformed opinions that created spikes of interest and outrage. For a long time there was silence. Then there was a quiet acquiescence from Big Pharma.

WARNING: PURE SPECULATION TO FOLLOW.

Could it be the pharmaceutical companies found a way to provide ARVs at an acceptable cost AND recoup their research costs by taking the long view? That is, sell the vaccine by the car-load to the World Health Organization and others at a price that would yield a minimal profit. Sell it in mas-sive quantities. Get entire populations on the medicine. Then recoup the research costs over the next ten or twenty years as the market – the infected populations – grow exponentially. If people wouldn't die from the disease but would continue infecting others, market growth in terms of millions of doses provided was guaranteed. What an elegant solution... appear to be humanitarian but ensure future profits for decades to come. Brilliant. Or have I just joined those who dream up corporate conspiracies that prey on the third world?

At least one pharmaceutical company has, in fact, persevered to find the closest thing yet to cure for HIV. Pfizer, Inc. has led the charge in combating the disease especially in Uganda where it funded and built the Infectious Disease Institute at Makerere University, a state-of-the-art clinical care facility that today is training healthcare workers, providing treatment to people living with HIV/AIDS and is conducting research to strengthen protocols of care. Opened in 2004, the building was the first significant addition to the campus since 1965. Having this facility has given Pfizer a front-line look at the disease and its treatments, information that has led to the release of what it calls the UK427-857 CCR5 blocker. "As the next generation of AIDS vaccine," Pfizer says. "CCR5 works with ARVs to become an HIV entry inhibitor."[39]

Microbiologist Donna Hacek of NorthShore University Health System in Chicago explains: "The blocker attempts to prevent the HIV virus from entering a healthy cell and damaging its immunology; ARVs do much the same. However, as far as I can tell, even with CCR5, the virus is never gone. The patient just gets to very low levels of organism, sometimes even levels below the detection limits of some test systems. But the virus is still there. A term we hear often – and one used as a gauge until we develop an actual HIV-killing virus

---

39   http://www.medscape.com/viewarticle/555524

is infectivity – how well does this medicine get us to that level of presence in the system where the HIV virus no longer has the power to infect healthy cells. There might be studies out there that have shown that infectivity rates are less once you get to a certain lower virus level but I doubt that without the virus actually being killed, that infectivity ever goes to zero.

"The HIV virus gets into cells, takes over and replicates itself," Hacek said. "It essentially hijacks the cell, sets up headquarters and takes over the business of the cell and says 'now you will make more virus.' I believe it destroys the cell in the process and this is how the legions of virus are able to infect more cells. Even when you are taking drugs, the virus gets into some cells because the virus is never completely gone. Blocking the virus from entering cells as CCR5 promises to do is a powerful new weapon in the battle as tests show it slows the production of virus and presumably, reduces infectivity. Nonetheless, the virus is never harmless, even when CCR5 and ARVs are present."[40]

"It all comes back to the basics," Ssempa said. "The spread of AIDS is a behavior problem. If people want to live a long life and not be the carrier of death for other people, they need to abstain from sexual relations until they are married. People who want to be married need to get tested for HIV status. HIV-negative couples need to be faithful to each other during their marriage, meaning have sex only with each other. If one or both parties in a couple are HIV-positive, they need to talk seriously and at great length about their sexual future including the reality that they should not have children. If they decide to marry, they must commit to being faithful AND take precautions between them.

"The challenge we have is providing constant, unceasing information and inspiration," Pastor Ssempa said. "The first real information I saw on AIDS came from an American medical missionary named Richard Goodgame who was teaching at the university medical school. He was one of the team that reported the causes of the disease to His Excellency in 1986. Goodgame created a pamphlet that showed how having sex with one person really meant you might be having sex with an entire village. Not long after I saw that material, I got involved by writing a drama about the path I was on... a fellow in party mode meets a girl and falls in love... meaning he's having sex with her. But he has a Christian friend telling him it's not the right thing to do. Our hero rejects that advice and listens to witch doctors instead. Then he uses double-condoms thinking that if one condom is 80% safe, two makes him 160% safe. Everybody laughs. In the end, the fellow regrets his promiscuous lifestyle and plans to give his life to Christ but he dies before he can commit. We left the challenge to the audience. What about you? The play got recorded and passed around a lot. Did we make a difference? A girl named Erina came up to me a few years ago and told me her story. She had a boyfriend who had money. He bought her telephone air time and drove her around in his Pajero. But when she saw the drama she realized how much she was at risk and she cut off the relationship. This story encourages me because she made her decision not based on whether the man had a condom in his pocket but on wanting a lifestyle pleasing to God."

Pastor Ssempa was not alone in trying to reach young people with the abstinence and being faithful message early on. Andrew Mwenge, the Senior Pastor at Kampala Baptist Church recalls wrestling with the issue in the 1980s. "There were many sexual issues that had come up over the years, especially a sense of apathy about relationships. The common thread, especially among young ladies, is you cannot trust men. Many of them have grown up with parents in polygamous relationships so they might find out they have a sister of a late age and so there was a lot of distrust. Then AIDS came on the scene. And so we wondered – how do you make massive impact in the thinking of the young people on the subject of sexuality. We had just come back from a conference in Zimbabwe where we heard a presentation from one of the people who had started a program called True Love Waits in the US. He shared his experiences and we thought it was something we could use.

"We launched our own version of True Love Waits in 1994, to send young people one message: think about sex in context of your whole life's dream. It wasn't just 'don't do sex,' but how does it fit into your dreams for a family, your dreams for a life? We challenge people to think about how a sexual act might interrupt a productive life.

"Designed as interactive dramas, the program started by asking people to draw a picture of what their family might look like. We put two people together like Adam and Eve and then they draw in children, extended family. Then we ask a lot of questions, "How many partners do you think a typical Ugandan youth will have by the time they get married? Could it be five? ten? twenty? Using that picture, we paint a scenario where a person tries one partner, but they're not satisfied so they try another. We line them up behind him. Then we try another we call Sarah, but he doesn't realize Sarah has had sex with James. So any problems Sarah and James had come into the picture. So we end up with a lot of people in the line. Then we ask the questions, "what kind of problems do you think might be in this line? Emotional problems? AIDS?"

At the end of three or four hours, the young people have several of these visual images in their head. Then we open things for discussion and, I have to say, we always get good questions from the heart. In the end, we ask everybody to leave the room and invite only those who are willing to make a commitment to abstinence to come back. There is usually a minimum team of four counseling in the hall. People do not feel those who stayed out are not rejects. People have a chance to make a decision and sign a card. They sign two; they keep one, we keep one. We celebrate with those who have committed."

I had to ask: did it work? Did you reach young people?

"Well," Pastor Mwenge said. "We've been at it for more than ten years with aggressive training in only three. The training would have continued but we did not have the funding. When we were fully equipped, the program sent ten teams of youth workers going up country where many NGOs wouldn't go. We spoke to over 150,000 young people and have over 75,000 signed commitment cards. We still have them on file."

Those are impressive statistics, I said.

"Well, Mzee, they are, but we have a lot of young people failing. If you think about it from purely a purely human point of view, I understand the objection: Abstinence is not realistic. It does not work. Some of our own team members have failed, not many, but a few. So others look at us and say, "didn't we tell you?" We have to admit it: the easiest choice is to be careless. It's hard. I have to make the choice every day to be faithful to my wife. Life is full of tough choices. It's difficult to engage the brain over the body. The concern is that if you just tell them abstinence is the only answer they may fail and then you want to give them the condom option, but then it's a choice between the hard and the easy and they choose the easy. As clergy, we have those debates and I can appreciate them, but we try to hold people to a standard where, even if there was no AIDS, this is what God wants for us and I think for me, that's what separates me from others that are interested in watching less people die. I have more than just death on my mind." [41]

The first opportunity I had to speak directly to a young person on this subject was at the home of my friend Denis Ndyabawe in Kampala who, as part of his work with The Navigators, held a weekly Bible Study for students in his living room. He introduced me to Sandra Mbanga a secondary school student at Makerere College. I asked her: "What do young people, you and your friends, think about abstinence and condoms and sexuality?

She replied candidly: "The kids I know are very sexually active. Those who talk or even believe in abstinence are regarded as weird." She laughed. "We live in the moment and don't worry about the future. If a condom is 99% effective, then it's worth the risk. Being faithful is a good thing. If I have a boyfriend and I am faithful to him, then I am limiting myself and my risk. But, with ABC, if we are told these are our choices, we will always take the C. And with the government providing condoms, the kids think it's okay."

Listening to this exchange, Denis chimed in. "Yeah," he said. "When I was growing up, people with AIDS were segregated like lepers. People were afraid of the disease. I got saved in 1985 and, to me, since abstinence is mandated in the Bible,

41   Interview, Andrew Mwenge at Kampala Baptist Church, January 22, 2005

it was part of the package for being saved. I was abstinent until I got married. It was not easy, but I kept telling myself, "I have a good bargain with God. Why would I betray Him?"[42]

Pastor Ssempa echoes this sense of purpose: "For years now I have been telling these things to young people on college campuses and through my radio program," he said. "We sponsor concerts like the Ignite Campus Festival featuring people who have turned from living evil lives to living for Christ – like Roger Mugisha, a former Satanist known as DJ Shadow. We gave out 15,000 Bibles to freshers (first year university students) this year. Sometimes I feel like I am shouting into the wind. But there are enough people who understand and believe and care that it makes this work worth it. Still, today, despite ARVs, I am sure each of the young people in this audience knows someone who has withered away and suffered into death from AIDS. I will keep going until I can't speak anymore. This is the issue of our age. It is a perfect platform for talking about obedience – obedience to God's commandments, obedience to the things Jesus expects of us – of behaving in a way that is pleasing to God.

"Our kids can go through True Love Waits," he said. "They can sign the card. But what happens then? Every day, everywhere young people look, the message is to go have sex. MTV says you've gotta have sex to be popular. The condom billboard says go ahead, have sex, it's safe. In the music, in the movies the message is you've gotta have sex. But I say the church and the parents and the teachers and the counselors need to say no. The truth is God has a plan for you. And promiscuity will

---

42   Interviews, Sandra Mbanga and Denis Ndyabawe at Denis' house in Kampala, January 15, 2005

kill you – first in spirit, then in body. This message needs to be sent as often as MTV. It is a God-sized job."

Walking out of the swimming stadium after Pastor Ssempa's presentation, I could not help but hear the buzz of conversation among his listeners. They were debating what they had heard, parsing his words, retelling the stories. As a group, they were excited, refreshed and hopeful. At the gate, I was handed a pamphlet for an Abstinence Rallye with the keynote speaker First Lady Janet Museveni to occur in approximately two weeks. More than 2,000 young people were expected to attend. I found out later more than 10,000 showed up. Here we were, nearly two decades years after the President defined the solution to "the behavior problem," delivering the same message to yet another generation. I wished I could have attended that rally. I pray Pastor Ssempa is preaching by the pool on Saturday night.

# The Role of the Church in the Battle Against AIDS

*"When we put our hands and our heads together, we save lives."*
- Rev. Fr. Dr. Joseph Obunga

If one should ever wonder about the role faith can play in beating back the AIDS epidemic, one need only go to Uganda to see the results firsthand. There are not many documented examples of such a thing. Google the subject and you will not find much. Yet faith applied in the forms of education and direction from the indigenous religious community, relief brought by more than 400 faith-based non-government organizations, and support from numerous foreign churches, missionaries and foundations has been a critical factor in bringing the insidious disease under control here.

"Faith-based organizations (FBOs) have a really important role to play in stopping the spread of AIDS and they've been sidelined," said Harvard's Ted Green.

FBOs have been working for behavior change – pushing AB, abstinence and being faithful, since before Uganda's official AIDS initiative began. They have been working with orphans and the sick and the dying and the bereaved but they haven't been funded to work in AIDS prevention. Ignoring this very important factor of public health policy has no doubt cost millions of lives."

President Museveni mobilized churches to broadcast the "Zero Grazing" and "AIDS Kills" messages because, as he said, it was "the fastest way to reach the greatest number of people in all the corners of the nation." For most of the people in this rural society, church is the center of their moral and social life. With few distractions – television, movies, the Internet – going to church and church-sponsored events meets the human need for pleasant, meaningful interaction. Sunday school and Bible studies are social events that teach morality. Likewise, the leaders of churches are looked upon as the moralizers, the people who put life's trials into perspective, the mediators in family disputes, the respected repositories of God's word. So when preachers began to talk about AIDS from the pulpit, people listened.

The strongest early voice in the battle against AIDS came from the Roman Catholic Church, the largest single religious entity in Uganda. Not only is the church populous in its congregations, but a large percentage of the schools in the nation are parochial schools under Catholic direction and more than half the hospitals in the nation are Catholic. Moreover, the Roman Catholics in Uganda work closely with church leadership from surrounding countries, giving it a regional perspective.

I had a chance to speak with Rev. Fr. Dr. Joseph Obunga, the Secretary General of the Catholic Secretariat at his offices in Kampala in 2005. "From the beginning, we have tried to teach people that abstinence is the only sure way to avoid problems from sexual activity," he said. "All the religious schools here are the same – Catholic, Muslim, and others. You won't find condoms on our campuses, but it is getting harder to keep them away.

"The Catholic church has been actively involved with fighting this disease since 1989 with our first pamphlet called *The AIDS Epidemic*," he explained. "Later, we started a program called Save the Youth from AIDS. It is still a common topic in schools. And we organize regional conferences to keep the dialog going. The local churches have the power to energize people. When we put our heads and our hands together, we save lives. These days we regularly organize field trips from one parish to another called 'exposure trips' so people can learn from one another. This is what the church is supposed to do – it is people loving their neighbors as themselves."

Working alongside Fr. Obunga at the Uganda Catholic Secretariat is Ron Kamara, who chairs the HIV/AIDS committee for the Interreligious Council. This organization acts vigorously to be a common point of information gathering and dissemination for all the religious entities in Uganda – Catholic, Evangelical, Muslim and any other interested parties. "The AIDS environment changes almost on a daily basis," Kamara said. "There are often new complications, new drugs and treatments, new interactions with prescription medicines. Today's infections are different than those of ten years ago. And, we now have drug abuse to factor in. There are also problems with the mythology of condoms, the supply, the usage, the quality. We report the mixed messages being made by independent NGOs. And where we find programs and resources that are helpful, we pass the word. We keep our data fresh. We are a vital resource. I like to think people get government information from us before they get it from the government.

"We are being aggressive with our information management because we have seen a reduction in infection rates," Kamara said. "Once people know the facts, they can act."[43]

With the strength of the Catholic Church in Africa and its emphasis on experience sharing through regional conferences, I asked Fr. Obunga how he thought the Uganda Model could be spread to the rest of Africa. He said, "We had an Africa-wide conference in South Africa in 1999. By then, the disease had killed millions of people. Many of the representatives there thought the Americans were going to come in and solve the problem medically. They are still waiting. And people are still dying. I guess I don't have a good answer to the question except to keep meeting and keep talking."[44]

In September of 2007, Bishop Hugh Slattery of the South African Diocese of Tzaneen spoke about the current state of AIDS prevention through pro-life Population Research Institute's Weekly Briefing. "Only one African country, Uganda, has successfully combated AIDS," he said. "The unsung hero of Uganda's victory over AIDS is a Catholic nun by the name of Sister Miriam Duggan, M.D. Early on in the fight against this deadly disease [the 1980s], Sister Miriam developed a program called *Education for Life*, a program which encourages people to be abstinent before marriage and faithful within it. By educating people about the dangers of promiscuous sex and its deadly consequences, this program helped to change the mindset of many Ugandan people. The adult HIV rate in South Africa was 18.8% at the end of 2005, or about what it was in Uganda 15 years ago. *Education for Life* has now been

---

43   Interview, Ron Kamara, Chair, HIV/AIDS Committee, InterReligious Council, at Secretariat offices in Kampala, January 18, 2005
44   Interview, Rev. Fr. Dr. Joseph Obunga, January 18, 2005 at his offices in Kampala

introduced in this diocese and is spreading throughout South Africa."[45]

One can only wonder why it took the South Africans so long to put that tool to work.

As vocal as the Roman Catholics have been about applying "The Uganda Model" Africa-wide, the Anglican Church of Uganda has been even more persistently loud. Over bowls of *bushera* at his home one morning, Archbishop Henry Orombi told me, "The Church of Uganda is clear in its theology of passion. Nationwide we speak to young people especially those 13-25 years old to let them know their sexuality is God's gift to them. We want them to make a decision to work with God's will and to realize that AIDS is not a disease but an attack on faith. We teach that condoms give artificial permission for people to take relationships beyond what God wants. We also show people how to have compassion for those who are infected and for them to be accepted by society. The more we can show them compassion, the longer they will live. But the essence of our AIDS education is *it will get you* if you are not diligent.

"Not all of the countries in Africa were very serious to begin with," the Archbishop added. "In Malawi, it was not easy for churches to speak out. Other places like South Africa did not accept that AIDS should be something to talk about because culturally there are a lot of taboos associated with sex. Kenya didn't want rumors of disease to hurt its tourist trade. Those places are having raging epidemics even today. Our position was not embraced by everybody but people are beginning to realize that our current position is about the safest way we can

45   Population Research Institute, Weekly Briefing, September 17, 2007 http://www.pop.org/main.cfm?id=307&r1=2.00&r2=1.50&r3=0.02&r4=0.00&level=3&eid=1110

address AIDS as a church. We have a common name for it. We have a common belief in church relationship with the people.

"The ironic thing about this curse," Orombi said, "is that the major transmission is through sexual relationship which is the passage of life for us. Why would it attack there? You really need to know Satan is playing a very serious role here, attacking at the very temple of making life and turning it into a vehicle for death.

"In the context of the continent, I think in the last few years, we have not begun to speak about AIDS *per se* but in 2000 I was in Cape Town and the church there was asking me if they could come to Uganda and learn from what we have learned. I said 'Yeah, Man. Give us an opportunity and we can show you.' That was recognition of needing some help. Well, they came and were in contact with Rev. Canon Gideon Byamugisha who referred them to Church of Uganda Services. I never heard what happened."

I had read much about the popular and controversial Rev. Byamugisha, the first Anglican priest to publicly admit having contracted HIV and had certainly heard opinions of the cleric from Rev. Martin Ssempa.

Anglican cleric Byamugisha apparently learned of his HIV status in 1992, only weeks after the death of his first wife who died suddenly and was later determined to be HIV+. When asked, he says he cannot be sure when he contracted the virus, but that it may have come as the result of a transfusion with tainted blood. To this day, he sadly admits he may have transferred the disease to his wife. Rev. Byamugisha has since remarried to a woman who is HIV+. In public appearances before the U.N. General Assembly, at AIDS conferences around the world and in his parish in Uganda, the media presents him as something of a church rabble-rouser because he includes condoms in the abstinence and being faithful set of solutions offered by the church.[46] Rev. Byamugisha has never responded to any my persistent requests for an interview, but I asked Archbishop Orombi if Gideon's message causes problems with the church's emphasis on abstinence and being faithful.

"I would not say Gideon is misrepresenting the church," Orombi said. "We must allow matters of degrees when people talk about ABC. Some will talk more abstinence, some more on being faithful, some more condoms. The Anglican Church has no problems with married people using condoms in their context of being faithful to each other. And some people will never be A or B so what do we do with them? We need to urge them to use every weapon available to fight this disease and we need to keep talking. Gideon is very good at that. We also say, if you're living outside of God's will, you are dead already. Maybe your skin will still be alive another two or three years, but that's not what you are. You are more than your body. We want to be very strong about that."[47]

"We first noticed the effects of AIDS in the congregations," said Canon Benoni Mugarura, now retired as the senior pastor at St. Francis Chapel, Makerere University. "We saw the wasting away of the flesh from week to week but it was mysterious. Nobody knew what it was so they called it "slim," with people becoming thinner and thinner until they were finished. When we finally found out what caused the disease, we as church people really didn't know what to do. People were afraid to admit they had the Slim. They would keep it as a family

46   http://www.abc.net.au/rn/religionreport/stories/2006/1697057.htm
47   Interview, Archbishop Henry Orombi, January 21, 2005, at his offices in Namirembe, Kampala

secret because if they admitted they had the disease they were admitting they were sexually active, sinners. It was a stigma. When the government went public with it, we all suddenly felt we had permission to speak about it as a problem larger than our selves. We stopped using a common chalice for Holy communion. We openly spoke about it from the pulpit and the message resonated because, after all, people we knew, people we were close to were dying from the sin of promiscuity. We founded an organization called Anglican Youth Fellowship with a choir that would go out to do concerts and share their experiences with Christianity. These kids had a huge influence on their peers at a time. They were saying 'We are university students. We are having fun. We are full of life. We are with Christ. We are abstaining and we are not missing anything.' That was powerful.

"When I came to this University there were 4,000 students," the Canon said. "Today, 20 years later, there are more than 40,000 and there are other universities all over the country. After all this time, the behavior message is beginning to sink in. Students are clearly aware that if they are sexually active, they are at risk of getting HIV/AIDS. Therefore, more and more of them are simply deciding to mind school. If you add the two groups – the people who mind their lives as Christians and the people concentrating on school instead of sexual activity, that will make up a far larger majority than those who are careless. This is progress.

"For the world to deny that Christianity has had an effect on this epidemic is sad," Canon Mugarura said. "We here in Uganda are fortunate that we had the East Africa Revival in the 1930s, an event that continues to influence our society, so much so that even though people don't know, they are living the effect of that. Prior to the Revival, immorality was part of the society where brothers lived with each other's wives and sometimes fathers had sexual relations with their daughters-in-law, widows were like public wives if they were not taken on by the brothers-in-law as part of the inheritance. All these things were ingrained in the culture. The Revival caused immediate change.

"Where those cultures survived, especially in other countries, people died – and continue dying to this day. The church is in those places, but you see instances where the President of South Africa lost a child to AIDS while the Anglican Archbishop denies the country has a problem, calling AIDS 'a disease of the poor.' In 2000, we were in South Africa and Archbishop Donani was still denying it. I remember talking to a group of clergy who were totally frustrated with the position of the church and the position of the government because the people in the parishes were dying. The result was like we saw here 20 years ago – AIDS was a private disease. People were and still are being stigmatized to death."[48]

For a non-University perspective, I spoke to Rev. Zac Niringiye, an Anglican Bishop at his offices in Kampala. Ben introduced me to his spiritual mentor as Mzee Twesigye. "*Twesigye*," he said with a little laugh. He looked into my eyes. "I like that."

Then he grew serious. "When it comes to AIDS, for me, it is a personal pilgrimage. I think for many people in the West, AIDS is a theory, *their* disease. But it is not a theory at all. It is a story we are living out today. My own brother had the disease in the mid 1980s. At that time, there was very little information

---

48   Interview, Rev. Canon Benoni, Retired Sr. Pastor St. Francis Chapel, Makerere University, at his home in Kampala. January 17, 2005

about AIDS and the church had a 'holier than thou' attitude.
For me, when I saw my brother, he looked dreadful. Emaciated. Even as a Christian man I could not embrace him. I was
afraid of him. It was a painful personal conversion to give up
my comfort for the sake of my brother, AIDS or no AIDS and
I decided to embrace him. In that moment, I realized this is
what we all needed to do - embrace all those in need and treat
them as brothers and sisters.

"I salute the leadership in this country that took action
to stop the disease because, as you heard Canon Benoni say,
once the government showed us the way, we had permission
to take action. But I have to tell you, the man who influenced
the President to approach the churches – rebuke them for not
paying attention to their dying congregations – was one of our
Bishops, Misaeri Kauma, from Namirimbe, a man who had
lost a brother to the disease, who welcomed people into his
church and set a new standard of Christian care. The churches
woke up when they realized their own people were dying.

"We started a program called FOCUS/HIV/AIDS Operation Rescue where we and people from Scripture Union part-
nered with five churches, five secondary schools and five
colleges. We quickly became part of the noise reaching people
about the cause of AIDS. Later we started Christian Strategies
for HIV/AIDS Prevention and Care, a counseling organization
telling people about the realities of condoms. In the course
of this work, *we found 60% of university students said they
wanted to know how to manage their life rather than just use
a condom.* This set the direction for our work throughout the
1990s.

In 1991, we showed a film from Life Ministries, which is
the name for Campus Crusade in Uganda, called *Who do you*

*listen to?* It told the story of a student and how he ended up in a sexual situation. We showed it around and the students were amazed "That's how it happens," they said. It was powerful. Students identified with it. Out of the 8,000 people we showed it to, we got over ten percent to sign up to join accountability groups. "We are happy to study the bible, to be able to know how we can live lives that are responsible" they said. These are significant, ongoing programs started by and perpetuated by the church."[49]

"The Bishop is correct... AIDS is a very personal story for us," said Rev. Frank Isingoma, an associate pastor at All Saints Cathedral in Kampala, when I spoke to him in 2005. "I was saved by God's grace because, in our family, my mother delivered 16 children to my father. My step mother delivered two more. Out of that there were three sets of twins. Today, most of my sisters are widows because of AIDS. Most of my brothers-in-law who died left at least three kids each. Of the 16 kids in my first family, only six are left. In my father's family we have lost 20 people. I am now shouldering 13 kids for school fees. And I am not alone. There are many people in this congregation who regularly support five, six, eight kids either in their homes or in school.

"I think we are making progress," he added. "Virginity at marriage is on the increase. People are getting more confidence about denying condoms. They hear from our President to put your hope in yourself, not in a condom. Be faithful. A condom is your last choice. Abstain. Morality is on the rise. The message is: *with sexual immorality, you are finished.*

---

49    Interview, Bishop Zac Niringiye at his offices in Kampala, January 21, 2005 – Doc. 55?

"Personally, I have three daughters and a son. I addressed sex and health issues with all of them early on. I am assertive. I told them to stand on their own, to think for themselves. I met their boyfriends and girlfriends and talked to them the same way. They didn't like it. But I kept asking myself if I was doing the right thing or the wrong thing, but I did it anyway. I think they must have listened to me because they are at university now and they are still alive."[50]

When Rev. Isingoma finished his story, I could only imagine what it would be like to be a parent of teenagers in this environment. You have done your best to raise them. You have alerted them to the dangers, more than once, maybe too much. Now your child comes home sick. You know full well if someone is HIV+ they could die from any disease. You wait. You wonder. You pray. You cry.

One question kept nagging at me especially after speaking with both the Catholic and Anglican church leadership here: Why has the Ugandan Model not been applied across Africa? I needed to talk to someone with experience outside of Uganda. That's how I got to Oliniye Daramola, the African Regional Secretary for Scripture Union (SU) based in Nairobi, Kenya. Sitting on a tree-shaded terrace at Namirembe Guest House, the bougainvillea glared red against the hazy sky. Iridescent hummingbirds flit overhead. The table cloth had "I love Jesus" printed on it in a crazy-quilt pattern and there was praise music playing through small speakers throughout the complex.

I opened the conversation with my burning question: When the global AIDS organizations talk about Uganda, they are complimentary about the progress that's been made here

50   Interview, Rev. Frank Isingoma, All Saints Church, Kampala, January 7, 2005

but none of them mentions the role the church has played in those results. Yet we know that role has been huge. So I'm wondering, if a strong Christian and church influence works in Uganda, why isn't it working in other places?

"I would say the first achievement in Uganda is the leadership did not hesitate to announce that it had a problem," Darimola said. "After that, it was a rather unique combination of willing partners in the churches, the schools and the government who were motivated to take a consistent message nationwide.

"Other countries were lacking one or more of these critical pieces," he added. "Kenya waited for over a decade to recognize AIDS because they didn't want to discourage visitors and the disease there got out of control. In Botswana, we were able to impact the schools but the church is not strong. In Nigeria, it was in 1998 or 1999, one of our pop singers, "Kuti" (Fela Anikulapo-Kuti) whose name means "I have death in my pocket," married 27 wives in one day before he died of AIDS. Only then did the Minister of Health acknowledged the AIDS problem in a public announcement. In South Africa, the government ignored the problem. But even there, a new study sponsored by Squibb just showed that kids in schools touched by Scripture Union exhibit a markedly different attitude toward sex."

I asked Olinye about his experience in Muslim countries to see if there was any faith influence over AIDS there.

"Muslim countries seem to have lower AIDS rates because of the strict rules of Islam," he said. "In Egypt, they say they don't have a problem but I think it is hiding in Cairo just as it is in any big city. We have strong ministries in Senegal and Mali because they welcome the help, knowing we are working to save the lives of their children. In Northern Nigeria,

Christianity is not allowed so we must make the moral message. All these things have some influence."

So, I queried: Would you say Uganda is a kind of magic
combination of motivation and leadership that is hard to find
in other places.

"Exactly," he replied. "God blessed Uganda when she
needed it the most."

Olinye was called to another meeting. Ben ordered a pot
of African tea and sat back in his chair, clearly moved by what
he had heard. Then he said to me, "Mzee, I have to tell you,
as someone who has lived through the worst of the AIDS era
and as someone who worked with Scripture Union for more
than ten years, I can only say that my brother Olinye and Pastor Ssempa and His Excellency and the Archbishop and the
many others we have talked to are all correct. Behavior can
be changed. Just as children can be taught to not put their
hands in the flames of the cooking fire, children AND adults
can be taught to take equal care with their sexuality. The Bible
tells us how Paul changed people's behavior in many places;
entire cultures were affected in Colossi and Thessalonica and
Rome. The idea that sexuality is any different than any other
behavior, which apparently is the premise of the world's public
health authorities, demeans our humanity. People of the third
world – the Africans, the Indians, the Khazaks, the Haitians,
the Hondurans – all of whom are our brothers and sisters in
Christ - do not need to be managed like pets or cattle. They
need to be informed of their options, taught about the spiritual
and physical consequences of their actions and given a higher
purpose for life than having sex. These things can be done by
churches and caring governments and NGOs equally. Looking
at Uganda, it doesn't seem like such a difficult thing to do."

# The Hope: Hidden Treasure

*"I want to be a doctor."*
- Obadiah Monday

Deep within the tragedy of AIDS, muffled beneath the noise of governments and social engineers, standing still in filthy clothes, with rheumy eyes, clinging to a chain link fence that separates tragedy from opportunity are thousands and thousands of orphan children who want nothing more than the chance to go to school. "Please, please, Mzee, if you can just help with school fees" is a frequent plea I hear from young people wherever I go in Uganda.

These requests, as polite as they are, used to bother me. In Chicago, I had grown immune to the panhandler on the Madison Street bridge cadging quarters from commuters. I don't trust beggars on the bridge because there is always this feeling that my largesse is about to be spent on brown bag wine... and so, I rationalized, the kinder thing to do is to not contribute to a bad habit. But pleas from abandoned, feral children are different. I was one of those whose resolve was cracked one day and said, "Okay, I will provide school fees." Many others have done the same. And now, after more than seven years of watching orphan kids seize the precious opportunity with both hands, I can attest that these formerly lost ones are growing, maturing, and becoming larger than life adults. They are like hidden treasure and their achievements are nothing less than remarkable. The investment was worth it.

Consider these five cases:

### Ivan

A thin boy in his late teens, Ivan was always seen with a book in his hand but like many young men at his school, Ivan was always struggling to find school fees. He had a good mind for numbers and wanted more than anything else to learn computers but he could not stay in school if he did not have funds.

A sponsor answered his plea one day and began paying his school fees which amounted to $250.00 per year to cover tuition, books, uniform, room and board. Once freed of his financial burden, Ivan sailed through Secondary School, college and Kabale University to graduate with a degree in Information Technology. Less than four months later, the University had hired him to be a lecturer in the subject. He is now pursuing a master's degree while using his knowledge to bring computing infrastructure to very rural parts of the subcounty. Go to Facebook and search for Ivan Niyanzoma. He will be glad to chat with you and share his story.

### Obadiah

One year after a sponsor began paying his school fees in 2004, Obadiah was interviewed on tape saying, "I am doing well, 19th in a class of 43. When I am finished, I want to be a doctor."

His parents were both gone, leaving him to stay with his only relative, an Aunt in Kabale town. He worked to earn school fees in order that he could attend Secondary School on an island in Lake Bunyonyi. But the earnings were sporadic and he missed terms because he was busy breaking rocks or hauling goods for money. By age 20, he still had two years of secondary school to go. Yet here he was, enrolled full time thanks to a sponsor paying $250.00 per year for tuition, room, board, books and uniform.

Obadiah graduated from Secondary School near the top of his class. A year at college afterward did not go well but he persevered and, along the way, underwent six months of intense discipleship training at Juna Amagara Ministries. He also began to work in his home village as a sort of business development consultant teaching people how to wrangle bees and harvest honey and became inspired to go back school. Thanks again to his sponsor, he went to veterinary college and, after two years, graduated as a Junior Veterinarian. He had become a doctor after all.

Today, Obadiah works with his village and others to raise crops, create food products for sale and improve herds of goats, pigs and cattle which are the building blocks of wealth in this society. His smile is infectious. His faith is strong. He says he owes his success to God and a man who paid his school fees, a man he calls Dad. Facebook Obadiah Dasan.

### Isaac

The week Isaac joined the Juna Amagara orphan care ministry, both his parents had died. The 11 year-old was thin, very quiet, sad and bewildered about any future he might have. But he trusted one thing - the ministry people who came for him in the middle of the night would send him to school. Over time, he grew to be an active part of the orphan family and worked hard at his studies.

Six years later, a very mature, well-spoken Isaac was asked what he wanted to do after secondary school. "I want to be a lawyer," he said. When asked why, he replied, "There is too much injustice in the world. I want to be a part of making things better." This, from a child who just a few years before had no possibility that he might be able to choose his own path for a productive future. Upon hearing Isaac's story, a sponsor in the U.S., an attorney himself, stepped forward with the offer to pay for the young orphan's law school tuition when he was ready to enroll.

## Moureen

Tall and thin, she could easily be a marathon runner. Today, Moureen is a teacher, caregiver and location manager for a large orphan ministry in rural Uganda. But growing up, she too found herself unexpectedly alone, the head of a child-headed family of one when her parents died. Her life every day was one of survival, not only for finding food and shelter, but also hiding from grown men who are all too often sexual predators for girls.

She was taken in by an orphan ministry in her early years where she learned the love of a large family and had the chance to go to school where she studied Advanced level courses. Though no sponsor was available to send her to college, she was able to work her way though and earn a teaching certificate. Grateful for having been rescued from a life of hopelessness, she vowed to use her skills to mentor other children in similar circumstances. Today, she works in one of the most remote corners of the country mentoring orphan children after school and working with their guardians to improve their child care. When talking about her work, Moureen smiles and reports, the children who are mentored after school often find themselves at the head of their public school classes. "It is a good start," she says. "I am so happy." Facebook Moureen Kyokusiima.

## Herbert

Growing up in a very rural village of subsistence farmers, this young man was left very much alone after his mom died because his dad was mentally ill. He could have been fatally discouraged but instead was inspired to go to school because he had seen his uncle study hard, get scholarships and even study in America. The uncle whose name is Ben, was a student and ministry worker with little extra money but he saw the same fire in Herbert's eyes that he himself had had only a few years before. Whatever funds the uncle could spare went to pay Herbert's school fees. The young man excelled at university and graduated with a teaching degree.

Herbert was hired to work for a fledgling Uganda-run orphan ministry where he discovered gifts for organization and project management on a large scale. He particularly excelled at personnel matters, being attentive to individual needs but also making decisions for the good of the organization. He earned a Master's degree in Counseling. He married Sarah, the love of his life. They had a daughter, Pearl. And just recently, this young man, still in his 20s, stood as a candidate for Parliament from his local district. He did not win, but he says he is not finished either. Meanwhile, he fulfills a vital role as Operations Director at Juna Amagara Ministries, managing the schools, orphan homes and clinics that are the life line for more than 1,000 children.

Without help with school fees, this young man would most likely be a subsistence farmer today like his family before him. Instead, he is respected leader who magnifies himself every day and inspires the children who follow his example. Facebook Ainamani Herbert.

I walk away from these examples with a sense of hope for all of Africa when I see the intensity with which young people exhibit for an education. They are driven to make successful lives – as measured by how much good they can forge out for their fellow men. They are motivated to apply their energy and knowledge to touch as many lives as possible. The hardship of growing up poor simply anneals them into razor sharp instruments of change. Their success lets me set aside the tragedy AIDS has wrought because here, at last, is hope.

# PART III:
## Up Country

*"A man who has one finger pointing at another always has three pointing towards himself."*

*- African Proverb*

# The Mbarara Road

*"I make more money off furniture these days"*
- Coffin maker, Lyantonde

The day is bright and clear, a good day to go up country to Mbarara, the capitol city of the Ankole District. Business people and adventure travelers spend 10,000 Uganda shillings and four hours to make the trip by Jaguar tour bus. I prefer traveling by car because I often want to stop along the way, but it is the more expensive alternative at 100,000 shillings for gas and driver.

It takes special skills to drive the Mbarara Road. One really should be used to driving from the right hand seat, of course because things here follow the British system. Beyond that, you need lightning reflexes, the ability to judge the car's proximity to people on foot and bicycles, knowing where the speed bumps lurk and having nerves of steel as vehicles five times your size whiz by within inches of your window. I know these things because I learned firsthand these are skills I do not have.

Herbert is a young man I have come to know and regard as my good friend. He calls me *nshwento* - uncle. One day, Herberti retrieved me and my traveling companion from Ben's house in Kampala. We had appointments in Mbarara and, as usual, we were running late. From the back seat, I kiddingly urged Herbert to pass a slow mover, commented on his chosen speed and more than once, remarked about how gingerly we were traveling over the speed bumps. Ever the patient man, he listened and did whatever he thought was best.

When we stopped in Masaka at the popular take-away for a cold drink, he asked politely, "Mzee, would you like to drive?"

"Do I need a license?"

"Not really," he replied.

"Sure. I'll give it a whirl. How hard can it be?"

My first turn out of the parking lot was in the wrong direction and in the wrong lane. A few shouts and hand-signals from inside my car got us oriented and then we were off. The car was a stick shift with right hand drive which required shifting with my left hand. I drive stick shift cars all the time, but not in Uganda. It took a few miles, er... kilometers, to retrain the shift sensors in my brain to make my left hand understand an H pattern and still coordinate with my clutch foot. While all mental resources were focused on my left hand, I tried to concentrate on hugging the center line. Once or twice, the car moved off the line to the left and, more than once, my traveling companion, sitting in the passenger seat on the left, gasped as her door whizzed by an unsuspecting bicyclist with an inch to spare.

I discovered the hard way that speed bumps require skills not taught in the USA. Called humps, speed bumps here are often the size of small Alps. They are obviously intended to be a practical way to slow down traffic through congested areas, something a traffic light would do in the West, but without electricity, speed bumps offer a viable solution. I have noticed the speed bumps have grown in altitude over the years apparently because small ones apparently don't offer the drivers of large vehicles enough incentive to slow down. Yet these, like the one I faced while idling in the middle of the street as I plotted my climbing strategy, these are scarred by a thousand under carriages of cars that took them too fast. Take them too slow and you could get hung up, offering the local children a new seesaw for their recreational pleasure. We took the bump slowly and diagonally, successfully, but I wondered why there were not rows of muffler repair shops on both sides of each hump.

After twenty kilometers of driving the Mbarara Road, I was a nervous wreck. There was the driving, of course, and the near-misses, but it was the clenched jaw and the glowering looks from the girl riding shotgun that finally cracked my American élan. "Herbert, I give up. Would you please drive us the rest of the way?"

"Of course, Mzee," he said helpfully. In attempting to pull off the road to change drivers, I found a rare bit of shoulder where I could steer the entire car off the road. I hadn't calculated on the 12-inch drop off the pavement and we drove at about a 35 degree heel to larboard for more than a quarter mile. When we stopped, at least one "amen" rang into the sultry air.

Once again underway, I said, "Herbert, I will never again make a suggestion about your driving."

"Okay, Mzee," he said. "You can take the wheel whenever you want."

"Oh, look, there's a banana vendor," I replied. Herbert only smiled with that dimpled grin of his.

On another day we were zooming down the Mbarara road artfully skirting potholes, bicyclists and goats when we passed a roadside display of coffins. I begged Naris, my driver, to stop. "No, no, Mzee, we don't want to look at coffins," he said. "They are bad luck."

"But I want to see how they are made."

"But Mzee, they put dead people in there. It is bad luck." All it took was one remember-who's-bought-the-outrageously-priced-gas for this trip look and Naris reluctantly pulled over to the shoulder and backed up a quarter mile to the town of Lyantonde.

Naris told me that before AIDS, the word "coffin" was rarely spoken. Coffins were made by carpenters far from public view. Children rarely saw them even at funerals, since children did not attend burials. Twenty years later, there are coffin building specialists who have set up shop by the side of the road. Business is so good there is competition. Consumers can easily shop for price and quality. And on this day, in this place, children scampered over, on and around the display models set around the yard like so much furniture at a garage sale.

No simple pine box, these containers were shaped wide in the shoulders and narrow at the feet. The lids held small, framed windows, possibly to offer an eternal view to the outside world, but more likely to make it easy to identify the occupant when loaded coffins are shipped from town to town. They were stained in various tones and the varnish gleamed in the afternoon light. They came in sizes from infant to adult.

I asked the coffin maker, a tall, wiry, open-shirted fellow who was busy at work with his hand tools under a tin roof, "How's business."

"Oh, suh," he said. "People are dying to see me." He laughed.

"Old joke," I said. He shrugged.

"So your children are not afraid while they are playing around the coffins?"

"No," he said. "They don't know what people use these for. They are just boxes to them. Sometimes when people come to buy they are so sad, they have lost someone. They see the children here and they feel a little better."

"Do you think you would sell as many coffins if you were not here by the side of the road?"

"Oh, no. There is too much competition. I must be here by the side of the road."

"Are you selling as many coffins as you did five years ago?"

"No I'm not," he confessed. "There used to be five coffin makers on this road and we all sold four or five a day. But I tell you de troot, I hope for us coffin makers we are in a dying business." He roared at his own joke once again, head back and white teeth gleaming, clever fellow. Recovering himself, he added "I make more money off of furniture these days anyway."

"That's good."

"Yes, suh. That's very good. I am happy to be wukking."

I took a picture of one young boy in a raggedy red shirt making a funny face through the window of a coffin lid. Naris, watching from a safe distance, was glad to leave.

Charles (pronounced Char-less) was driving the day Herbert and a mixed vanload of missioners and Africans were gliding down the Mbarara Road. Herbert was oblivious to the sparse savannah drifting by the windows of the little

Toyota Combi bus; he had ridden this road so often, he no longer noticed the crows in the acacia trees, the zebras grazing beneath the power lines or the long-horned Ankole cattle spread across the brown grass. No, today, there were more important things. His head was bowed, his young brows wrinkled in concentration at the words he was reading. Someone had given him a book, *Things you Must Know Before You Get Married*. Though he intensely wanted to be married, he did not want to make a mistake. After all, he had kept himself pure for 22 years and he did not want to waste the gift he would make to the woman who would be his bride.

A fellow passenger in the seat next to him had been watching the young man's face for some time. Clearly, he was rapt in this book, but the seatmate could not see the name of its title. Finally, he could stand it no longer. He tapped the fellow on his elbow and said, "*Sebu*, are you in pain?"

"Oh," Herbert said, startled out of the book. His face relaxed, softened, and he replied with a bright boyish smile, "Did I look like I was in pain?"

"Yes, young man. You looked like you were trying to pass a whole mango." The two men laughed. "I am Godfrey," he added.

"Pleased to meet you, *Sebu*," Herbert replied. "No, I am thinking about getting married and so I am reading this book."

"Well," Godfrey offered after seeing the title. "Depending on who you talk to, that book is either way too long or way too short."

"What do you mean?"

"Speaking as a man who has been married for two decades, I would summarize the book in a few words... give the lady what she wants. However, if you speak to a man who's been married for five years or less, you'll hear endless tales of confusion and mystery encompassing the gamut of human interaction from moods to money to sex... enough to fill several books that size. What is the name of your girlfriend?"

"Her name is Sarah. We met at university. She is a very wonderful person."

"She is beautiful, of course?"

"Oh yes. Quite beautiful."

"Then have you asked her to marry you?"

"She knows I would like to ask, but her family is very traditional. I must negotiate with her father before I will be allowed to ask."

"Ah, this must be the bride price," Godfrey said. "And may I ask how much is the man is asking for the hand of his daughter?"

"That is one of the things I am trying to figure out. In her family's tradition, the father does not set a price, but waits to see what the anxious suitor is willing to offer. This book is all about feelings and interaction between two people. It says nothing about negotiating for the bride. If my offer is too low, the father will be insulted. He will tell his daughter who will also be insulted and she will think I do not love her. However, if I offer too much, the father will think I am a rich man and will either negotiate for more or he will tell me this daughter is not nearly worth that price and will offer me another... or he will suggest I try another family who may be more worthy."

Godfrey, raised in the city and wise in the ways of the world, looked at his young friend, mystified that such practices were still alive in modern Africa. "So, what do you think is a fair price for the fair Sarah?"

"Five cows," Herbert replied. "No more than six."

Godfrey was intrigued that you could get a bride with cows. "Why six?" he asked.

Herbert clearly had been thinking about this a long time. "Her sister, Violet, was married after the offer of six," he replied. "Violet was the oldest and therefore the most valuable. With her now married, Paula is the next oldest and therefore the most valuable. Sarah is next after that, so she is not the most valuable. Her father would like to marry Paula off first but if an offer comes along for Sarah, even though she is less valuable, he might demand more for Sarah than she is really worth... out of order, you know. No less than five. No more than six."

"Do you love Sarah?"

"I do."

"And does she love you?"

"I believe so. After all, it is she who gave me this book. And I can see love in her eyes. But it is forbidden for her to declare herself to me while she is in her village. If I took her to Kampala, she would gladly tell me. But we would need to be married before I could take her to Kampala. You see my dilemma?"

"I do indeed," Godfrey said, pondering the problem. "So, do you have these cows?"

"No," Herbert said wistfully. "I will have to go get them."

"Where will you get them? Are you a farmer?"

"No, I am a church worker. I will need to save my money."

"Can they be just any cows? Maybe like those out in the countryside there?"

"Pretty much any cows, yes," the young man said. "Healthy, of course, and they cannot be too old. And they cannot be lame. If I try to bring cows that are not acceptable, I may need to add a half cow to the price."

"Half a cow?" Godfrey's eyebrows and his voice did a British dip in disbelief.

"Yes. A goat is considered half a cow… but that is after the price is agreed. Am I making sense?"

Godfrey, frustrated with all this talk of bride prices and cows, said, "Herbert, we are talking metaphor here, aren't we?" He waited for a wry smile from the young man. "A hypothetical discussion held with the father to show respect for the father's blessing, right? We're not talking real, live cows, are we?"

Herbert looked up without smiling. "Real cows," he said. He could not have been more serious.

"Well," Godfrey replied, somewhat embarrassed. "It sounds like you have this all figured out. I'm glad *you* understand it. But, let me ask…what is your best price beyond which you will walk away from the bargaining table?"

Herbert answered without hesitation: "I have decided. Six cows. Six cows for Sister Sarah."

Godfrey pondered his own family. When his two sisters turned sixteen, they merely chose boys in the city. They had sex and then they were married. That was nearly twenty years ago, though the men long ago died of AIDS because they were not faithful. The girls, who both tested HIV positive, could have had many other men, but chose instead to throw their energy into business, running shops in Kampala. They took pride in their accomplishments as successful working widows and did not seem to miss the men very much. How much better it is for Herbert to have to work hard at honest labor to win the hand of his fair Sarah. Perhaps it will make his a true marriage, faithful in every way.

The Combi bus chased its shadow through the yellowing dust of late afternoon. The driver was rigid as he guided the vehicle down the laser straight road, his eyes anticipating every pothole or piece of debris that might cause him to veer. At a hundred and ten kilometers per hour, the warm equatorial wind buffeting through the open windows was welcome to the passengers.

Herbert looked up from his book. "There is only one problem," he said to Godfrey.

"Only one?" the seatmate said. "What is that?"

"I am allergic to cows."

Godfrey snickered. Herbert cracked a sidelong smile. And the two men broke into hysterical laughter.

Another day on the Mbarara Road a van was loaded with 12 missioners heading back to Kampala. We had been driving for two hours. The sun, beginning its afternoon descent, cast its reddening glow onto the face of Mansour, our Muslim driver as he stared straight ahead, his statue gaze never varying, his huge hands on the wheel. I was in the co-pilot seat on the left side. There had been much singing and laughter in the first hour of the trip, but the rhythm of the road and the heat of the day lulled the group into a drowsy peace. With my arm out the window and the red dust of Africa in my pores, clothes rumpled from days of travel and praise songs ringing in my ears, I was happy. There was no other place on earth I wanted to be at that moment.

Directly in front of us was a Jaguar bus, one of those two-story, air-conditioned long-haulers used to whisk tourists and the Middle Class cross country. As Mansour moved to one car-length behind the bus, it became a yellow skyscraper blotting out the sun. Mansour drifted to the right from time to time, wanting to pass the bus, calculating, deciding when to make his move. A drift and a return. A car whizzed by. Another drift and a return. A truck whizzed by. Then it was a drift and a surge of every ounce of power the overloaded Toyota van could produce and Mansour was committed, in the middle of the oncoming lane with a wall of yellow bus to the left. The road ahead looked clear but the van was making little progress in passing the bus. Everyone aboard was awake now. In the distance we could make out the tiny shape of a truck coming straight for us. A moment later, we could tell it was a blue truck. A moment later, a blue truck loaded with bananas – a good 40,000 pound load. We had not yet passed the bus.

It was alarming enough watching the road between us and the oncoming truck rapidly shrinking. Then I saw another oncoming truck trying to pass the banana man, a tanker. Gasoline. My hand crushed the grab bar on the door. Mansour never blinked. I had a brief, fleeting thought about this Muslim man being a suicide driver on a mission to wipe out a dozen Christian evangelists. Then someone in the back noticed the gasoline truck and said, "Oh, my." It would be spectacular: a four-way head-on collision.

We were almost past the bus with the trucks so close we could count the slats on their grills when someone sitting in the back row yelled, kidding but not really, "Here I come, Jesus!"

I swear at that moment the gasoline truck slowed and faded back behind the bananas, the Jaguar driver took his foot off the pedal and our van slipped into a slim pocket of safety in the left lane as two trucks whooshed by. Mansour never blinked. Or grimaced. Or moved his fingers. Or even shifted in his seat. He drove on. I turned to the 12 wide-eyed faces behind me and asked, "Does anyone want to stop and change pants?"

My friend Denis was in a car accident on the Mbarara Road, a place where there are no minor collisions. Denis used to own a taxi company and, if you have ever ridden with him, you know what it is like to drive in a NASCAR race. He's an engaging guy who can expound on the news of the day, take phone calls and weave around slow drivers or goats or people with pushcarts at blinding speed. On the day of his accident, Denis was driving his cousin and a pregnant friend to a wedding and they were late.

The Mbarara Road is the only paved road connecting towns in southwest Uganda to the capital in Kampala. Though it was renovated in 2010, on this day it was two narrow lanes with potholes strategically placed on the center line and there are no speed limits. Denis veered to miss a missing chunk of highway on the side and was greeted by an oncoming car dodging a pothole on the center line. When he woke in the hospital, he was told he had a broken leg and a wrenched back and also, sadly, that three people in his car died as did the driver of the car that hit him. He lost a cousin, a friend and her unborn child in mere seconds and was so distraught he never thought he'd drive again.

Confined to a rented hospital bed set up in his living room, Denis asked me if I would stop on my way to Mbarara to take photos of the wreck. Thus, we found ourselves in the town of Masaka. We turned off the main road and followed a narrow track through town to the police station where the wreck had been towed. In a yard about half the size of a McDonald's parking lot were a dozen silent testimonies to the risk of traveling the Mbarara Road: A school bus T-boned in half. A pickup with its engine pushed into the driver's seat. Impossibly contorted sculptures of twisted frames, crystallized glass, wheels lying at crazy angles like feet on broken legs. We found Denis' Toyota Corolla under a blue tarp. The whole structure was twisted around the driver's seat, a mangled memory that will haunt Denis forever. I made a joke about why anyone would put a tarp over such a pile of scrap metal but my driver, Naris, said, "Oh, Mzee, you can see the engine is still good. At least three hundred dollars if they keep it out of the rain." I took the pictures quickly, trying not to think of the blood and bone that had been removed from these wrecks, and we left. I asked Naris to take it easy on the Mbarara Road. He nodded at my stating the obvious.

A favorite stop on the Mbarara Road is the equator.

The equator, of course, is the line on a globe that bisects the planet. In Uganda, it is a yellow line across the road. There are places where you can stand and have your picture taken. There are gift shops selling goatskin drums and cow bone jewelry. You can get a bite to eat. For a few shillings, you can use the latrine.

Everyone has heard about the equator, but to actually stand on it is a mystical moment. Look to the right or look to the left and you are exactly the same distance away from the same spot on the other side of the earth. Follow the line for 24,901.5 miles and you will end up at exactly the same place you are now standing.

The first thing that passes through the foreign visitor's mind is "how cool." The second is "can it be real?" If you really want to know how cool and how real it is, there is a young man named Huntington waiting to prove to you that you are standing exactly half way between the north and the south poles. He has a funnel and a bucket of water which he will put to work for the equivalent of about three bucks. I have brought so many customers to Huntington, he and I really need to have a discussion about commission.

Huntington puts his funnel on a stand about fifteen feet north of the equator line painted on the road. He holds his hand over the bottom of the funnel and pours in some water. He drops in a flower petal, explaining that you must watch these to see what they do. He waits until the flower is motionless, then he removes his hand. The water swirls in a counter-clockwise rotation, spinning the petal round and round until the funnel is empty, much like the water swirling in toilet bowl prior to the big swallow. Then he takes the bucket and funnel to the south side of the equator line and goes through the same process. This time the water swirls clockwise. Everyone is duly mystified and impressed but Huntington is not finished. Now he takes his funnel and places it square on the line. When he removes his hand from the end of the funnel, the water gushes straight down. No swirl. Everyone applauds while Huntington welcomes everyone to the center of the earth.

There is a small store at the equator that sells hand-made paper goods: note papers, greeting cards, journals with hand-made covers and hand-tied bindings. I asked the owner, "How did you learn to make paper?"

"Oh, a lady from Canada came over and showed me," she replied as though the Canadian had just ambled up the street. "She brought some small equip-a-ments, spent two weeks here teaching me and now I have this shop."

And so she did. In one side of the building were tubs for making the pulp, screens for drying the slurry, bottles with dyes. Screens with future paper lay drying in the intense equatorial sun. Two women worked at a table cutting and assembling products. The other side of the building was the store where tourists drifted in and out.

"Is this your family?" I asked, looking at the people there.

"Yes, they all work here?"

"How is business?"

"It is OK. We work every day."

"And because of this work everyone has enough to eat?"

"Yes. It is OK."

"That is so good. I am happy for you."

"Yes, suh. We are very happy here."

We're two hours into our van ride on the Mbarara Road with two hours to go and suddenly we stop at a clutch of wooden shacks.

"Why are we stopping, *Owesheimwe*?" I asked Ben.

"We promised to deliver Bibles to these people, Mzee. They are just here."

A wooden board roughly painted with the words "Drum Works" is nailed to a tree next to one of the shacks. I had whizzed past this stretch of road a half dozen times and had wanted to stop but it seemed we were always short of time. As I looked around, there were not just a few shacks, but

dozens, each one festooned with hand-made goat skin drums
of all sizes, shapes and colors. At craft centers and gift stores
throughout Uganda and at the airport, you will see the drums
for sale, but this place is different. This is where they are made.

Back in the woods, men sit with machetes and scrapers
shaping chunks of exotic wood – sydra, musezi, muvule and
mahogany for the bases of the drums. It is said each type
of wood gives a different tone, a personality. The more personality, the higher the cost. Watch where you walk because
here and there, goat hides are being stretched between pegs
pounded into the ground. Tan ones, white ones, blotchy ones
which, if they were from cows would be from Guernsey or
Holsteins. More pegs stretch a woven fiber made from goat
gut and strips of hide.

To make a drum, one piece of goat hide is stretched across
the top of the shaped and hollowed log, another across the
bottom and the two pieces are tied together with the fiber
until they are taut top and bottom. Every one of these drums
rattles because inside is a pebble – to give the drum life, they
say. These drums can be 36-inches long or six inches long –a
size for any budget. And at this spot in the road it looks like
there are hundreds of families – maybe a thousand people –
making a living from this work.

"About six months ago a group of people from Chicago
stopped here to watch the drums being made," Ben said to me.
"Your friend Joel was one of them. He started talking to one
of the stall owners and simply asked him if he was a Christian.
The man said no, but asked how one becomes a Christian. Joel
told him it was a simple thing. All he needed to do was say a
prayer and read the Bible. But we have no Bibles in our language, the man said. Joel told him if he wanted to pray the

prayer now, he would make sure that everyone got Bibles. The man was overjoyed. Right there on Mbarara Road with the traffic whizzing by and the sound of machetes shaping logs for drums, the missionary and the drum maker prayed the sinner's prayer asking Jesus to forgive this man's sins and enter his heart, making him new in all ways. I saw the two men hugging and went over to see what was happening. Joel told me the news. We sang *tukutendereza* and the whole drum maker village was smiling.

"It took six months," Ben added. "But we now have two cases of Bibles in the *Rukiga* language for these people. That is why we are stopping."

It is not an odd thing for van loads of *Mzungus* to stop here. The drum makers know they will be gawked at and photographed. They welcome the attention but hardly show it, knowing the people who visit will probably buy one or more drums. But this day, they all looked up from their work when Ben found the man who had prayed Jesus into his life a few months before. They recognized each other and greeted each other with smiles and hugs. Two cases of Bibles were brought from the van and set at this man's feet. "See," Ben said. "God answers prayers and His people keep their promises." The man took one of the books from its carton, wrapped his rough hands around it and closed his eyes for a moment. Then he whispered something to a young man next to him. The lad dashed off, but soon returned with a dozen or so other people, men, women and boys in worn-out clothes and bare feet. The Drum Maker handed each of these people a Bible, perhaps the first new book any of them had ever touched in their lives. They were silent. Ben gave a little speech in *Rukiga* capped off by a prayer of thanksgiving and then, as usual, everyone sang *tukutendereza.* Each person shook hands with each other person, the soft, white palms of visitors embracing the hard leathery hands of the craftsmen and vice versa. We piled into the van and got back on the road. I looked back to see the people still stroking the covers of the books.

"Ben, what did you tell them," I asked.

"I told them these Bibles were a gift from God. That people the drum makers did not know and probably would never meet paid for the books out of their own wages because they wanted to share the message so much. I wanted to give the Bibles value. These people will use the books to teach each other to read. We will follow up with this community to do Bible studies from time to time. The important thing here is we promised to bring them Bibles and we did it. They now understand and believe God answers prayers and keeps His promises even though it can possibly take some time."

In another 30 minutes, we passed a colorful klatch of roadside stands – the vegetable market - the stool makers. And later still, the basket weavers. I wondered how many of those would welcome the gift of Bibles in *Rukiga*.

# Suburban Life

*We are only Noah and his wife, building an ark to save a lost generation of people."*
- Rev. John and Jolly Mulindabigwi

Eventually, we reach Mbarara, the second largest town in Uganda. This is cattle country, a hub of commerce, a banking center and a place where more than 20 colleges and universities operate to capacity enrollment. On entering the town, we are greeted by the statue of a large Ankole cow with its distinctive long antlers reaching like raised arms to heaven. The main road courses past rows of stores selling building materials, solar panels, groceries, clothing, books, CDs, computers, baked goods and cell phones. There is a large open-air market tucked just off the main street. At the pharmacy all drugs including Indian equivalents of controlled substances in the U.S. are sold over-the-counter. There are Internet cafes. There is a clothing district where women make dresses on treadle sewing machines and men smooth the finished goods with charcoal-heated irons. The Shell gas station offers petrol at 1700 shillings per liter – about $6.00 per gallon.

Our van needed brakes so we went to the auto repair district. For those of us used to clean service bays with hydraulic lifts, this was an eye-opener. Corrugated iron sheets separated plots of land, each an individual mechanic's shop, each filled with vehicles in various states of disrepair. The soil was soaked with motor oil. Rusty engine parts lay here and there. Energetic young men in greasy blue overalls and bare feet shouted back and forth. An engine revved. Someone was spray painting a vehicle in a wide-board shed back in the corner. Wilson, our favorite mechanic said they were very busy and suggested we leave the van for a day. We were running late as usual so we explained we could not leave it but we have someone with us who knows how to change brakes. Could we have a space in the mechanic's yard and borrow some tools to do the job ourselves? Well, if you want, he said, yes.

Within minutes, a half dozen blue-coveralled men pushed vehicles out of the way to make room for our van. They became like Operating Room attendants, asking Kevin, the *Mzungu* mechanic, what he would like – jack up the car? Remove the hubcap? They scurried about, preparing the patient. Kevin asked for tools. The nurses removed the patient's wheel. Kevin exposed the worn brake pads. Calls of "Engineer! Engineer! What do you need?" rang out. At the engineer's hands, the old pads came off. New pads appeared and were handed in. They were installed and tested. No less than nine young men eager to witness a new surgical technique hovered over the wheel absorbing every turn of a screw, every testing of a spring. The whole group rejoiced when Kevin finished with an Amen! In minutes, the wheel was re-mounted by an assistant. The car was lowered off its jack and we were on our way. The job cost twenty minutes and twenty dollars including parts.

The working environment may be crude, but vehicles continue to operate because improvisation is strong. New parts are rare and cost is always an issue. I had watched Wilson bring a Land Rover, parked for more than nine years, back to life. It didn't matter that there were weeds growing up through the gear box or that the tires were sunken into the earth up to the rims, the steering and gearing linkages were intact and, with fresh fuel in a plastic milk jug stoppered by a potato, the engine kicked over. After the rusted-out gas tank was replaced, the car became serviceable thanks to Wilson's magic.

When I am in Mbarara, I often stay at the home of John and Jolly Mulindabigwi. Like Dr. Amos's house, this home is concrete block and stucco with a metal roof. There is a separate building for guests and an office, complete with Internet access. Cooking, however, is done is a slat-board cook shed over an open fire behind the house. Food is prepared inside but it is cooked outside. The essence of rural Africa hits me when I see this arrangement because this society seems to be reluctant about emerging out of the old ways. Ancient tribal culture mixes with modern automation and conveniences in the largest cities and the smallest villages. For example: In the middle of Kampala, clothing is still laid out on bushes to dry. Cooking is often done outside of the main house over an open fire. People who can find a plot of land, even one square foot, plant maize or beans.

Living in it I understand more of the African culture, and a certain frustration within the people. There are those who are stuck in the old ways, those who are being dragged inevitably away from the old ways and there are those who want nothing to do with the old ways. In Mbarara, the roads in town are paved with tarmac but side roads are unpaved, rolly and rutted. It is not uncommon to see an impeccably dressed business woman in dark suit, cream blouse, high heels and briefcase, hair done just so, riding sidesaddle on a *boda boda* down a dusty lane. Large, beautiful Spanish Colonial estates are bordered by dusty tracks. Local access roads such as the one to Pastor John's house are so uneven, vehicle passengers need to hang on tight with both hands even at walking speeds.

The Mulindabigwis have six children with just the two youngest still at home. The others are at boarding school or are graduated. I toured Jolly's garden which was large and prolific. I watched the construction of a house being built for Mzee Glen, one of the few *Mzungu* homes in town.

I ask John: "Do you know Milton the Customs Manager?"

"I do. He goes to All Saints."

"Yes. I met him there last week. He offered to make me a citizen of Uganda. Can he do that?"

"I would put nothing past Milton," he said.

John once again asks me to sign the guest book, a custom we came to expect whenever we visited an office or a home. This one is filled with the names of people from around the globe. In fact, the Mulindabigwis host so many people, their neighbors have asked if they are running a hotel. "It is good to have so many friends, is it not?" he says.

It takes me a few days of being up country before my ear tunes to the language, a mixture of British English, African accent and local dialect with local word order. Taken altogether, the language is robust with much inflection and often much body language. Greetings are robust handshakes or, if someone has dirty hands, they may offer an elbow.

"Mawneen, Suh. I know it is ully but you wanted to get a fast start."

"We wish you sef junny."

"This is a pissful nation."

"Mzee," Ben's daughter Marvel told me, "Your hat is dutty." I didn't understand her at first which made her a bit frustrated with me so, being fully fluent in American English said, "All RIGHT. Your hat is Dur-tee."

"We will be picking some cloth-uz at the hour of twell-uv."

"Thang Gode we have finally reached an ajreement. It was tremendous wuk."

Someone gets my attention: "Mzee Lee?"

I answer, *Kwangye?*" (Yes, please?)

My friend Apollo was driving the van through the still-wide-open neighborhoods of Mbarara when I saw a field of low-growing bushy plants. "What are growing over there," I asked.

"Oh, suh, that is penis," Apollo replied. I'm sure my eyes shot wide open in surprise.

"Say again, Apollo? What is that crop?"

"Penis," he replied. "You know, like penis butter."

Then it dawned on me: "Are you saying peanuts? Like ground nuts?"

"Yes, yes," he said, amused and somewhat surprised that such an otherwise intelligent person had taken so long to grasp his words.

"Well, Apollo, my ear is still tuning to your way of speaking, you know," I told him. "And what I thought you said, the word penis, well, you know that's what they call the man thing."

He burst out laughing, actually had to stop the car until the convulsions passed. "And you thought we were growing them in that field?" he said again, laughing so hard tears ran down his face which got me going and I could not stop. In time, we regained some composure and he began to drive again, shaking his head. "Oh, suh," he said a moment later, "if we could grow those things, Uganda would be poor no more." We both burst out laughing and had to stop the car once again.

Other snippets:

"What do you know of pidg-mees? (Pygmy people who live near the Rwanda border)" "Oh, they are dutty like animals"

"Mind the humps."

"Oh, my goodness. Myself, I would not do that."

The universal answer is "yah." *Boda boda* guy, do you know where this building is? "Yah." He takes off in some direction and after ten minutes asks directions as he goes. Do you know where you are going, I ask. "Yah," he replies. It turns out he didn't understand the destination to begin with. Musta been my accent.

You will hear people in conversation where one will be talking and the other will intermittently say, "Ayyyy." What the second person is doing is acknowledging or agreeing with a shortened form of the word "Ego" (pronounced ay-go) which means "Yes, I see, tell me more."

I have been to Mbarara enough times now that people recognize me on the street. Rev. Sam runs across the street to shake my hand and wish me *Mukama asiimwe*" Michael the Internet Café owner waves. Monica, a single woman who has adopted two HIV+ girls smiles when she sees me; her daughters are alive today because we provided funds for some ARVs.

Harriet from the Amagara Children's Home rushes over to introduce me to her husband-to-be. "Are you sure he is the one?" I ask with Tobias standing there. She blushes. "Why, yes," she replies with wide smiling eyes. "Okay. Then you have my blessing." They clearly didn't need it but say they are grateful for a blessing from a Mzee.

I was being driven to John's house late one night when we stopped to drop two of our team at a home owned by Miriam, a city planner in Mbarara. I had always wanted to meet someone in charge of this seemingly chaotic place and so I asked, "Mbarara seems to be doing well."

"Oh, Mzee, the growth of the town is far surpassing the ability of the planners to keep up with it," she said.

"Do you have responsibility for the roads?" I asked.

"Oh, that's our engineer."

"What are the plans for straightening out the wrinkles in the roads?"

"We have petitioned the government for a machine."

Thinking like an American entrepreneur once again, I asked, "What if someone had a machine, would you pay him to iron out the wrinkles?"

"Those things are here," she said emphatically. "But they are too expensive, maybe a million shillings ($500.00) a day. Now we need to petition the government."

"Do you think they will buy you a road grader?"

"In time, maybe yes."

Not likely in your lifetime, I thought. I related how, after being pummeled in a car trying to make any speed at all over the roads here, we laughed out loud when we read a headline in the newspaper "Bad roads inhibit economic development."

Missing the irony completely, she scowled and said reporters always dwell on the negative.

I was a little irked with Miriam who struck me as very bureaucratic, a not-so-hard-working buck-passer, an unimaginative problem-excuser rather than a problem-solver who couldn't see the benefit to the town of paying a road grader $500.00 a day for five days to improve three main roads – that better traffic flow would increase town efficiency, the flow of goods, the safety of the people. A planner without vision is no planner at all. Did I say my American attitude was taking over? After I thought about it, I concluded that maybe, just maybe the people like their roads just the way they are. Nobody will ever get a ticket for drag-racing on the back roads of Mbarara – or dare to go faster than 5 mph for that matter. So rather than struggle against it, I have decided to look forward to my road massage while we are driving around. It feels so good when we stop.

Early one morning, John Mulindabigwi and his wife Jolly stopped by. "Mzee, let us go take a ride. I want to show you a special project." "BAM! Another pot hole. WHOA! We veered into the buffalo grass around a crevasse. YIKES! We blasted through a pond-size puddle and splattered a cloud of red mud across the county. We are on the road out of Mbarara on our way to Kamwenge.

For the first half hour, the road is deliciously smooth tarmac. A branch veers to the left and we take it. Twenty minutes later at the Tree Shade Hotel where a sign advertises "Cold Drinks Here" but where the Coke machine at the front door is not wukking, we drop abruptly off the tarmac onto a path of rutted red dust. John is driving.

We are going to Kamwenge to check on the progress of a vocational school Rev. John and his wife Jolly are building there. It seems in the 1970s, the bad times of Idi Amin, many people from Uganda fled for their lives south to Tanzania. That country did not welcome them, but it did not turn them back either and so the population settled in an open area not far from the border. In time, the refugee camp became a village with shops, streets, brick houses, schools, churches and farms. A generation of Ugandan children was born on foreign soil. However, shortly after the turn of the millennium, Tanzania grew tired of its visitors and expelled them back to Uganda. 30,000 people were forced to leave their squatter village with its wells and schools and cobbled-together self-sufficiency to start over – but where? The government of Uganda didn't want or need more refugees, but these were fellow country-men. There had to be a place for them.

The place chosen was a former UN-run refugee site near the town of Kamwenge, some 200 kilometers north of the border. There was plenty of space, but as a former site, all hous-ing, water supplies and sanitary facilities had been decommis-sioned, which meant these 30,000 would be literally starting from scratch. Both Jolly and John, who grew up near Kam-wenge and felt many of these people were part of their village, wanted to do something to help. The greatest need, John said, was for people to learn skills and ways to start useful enter-prises. His wife agreed and so the two sold a parcel of land Jolly had inherited and bought land near Kamwenge town for a vocational school.

The day was heating up. Meandering down the road, around the gullies and the goats, sometimes with short bursts of speed, but mostly being careful not to lose the wheels in muck, the undercarriage to rocks or the shock absorbers to surprise bumps, we passed through countryside that looked much like a raggedy Pennsylvania, a thousand shades of green patches rolling into a horizon of clear blue sky.

"Mzee," John asked. "Would you like to stop for the tree bathroom?" The side of the road was fine with me, but, before I could answer, the ladies in the van said, "That would be nice." He stopped just past a clear, swift-running river next to a glade of large trees. The ladies meandered into the woods, the sway of the dresses, the majesty of the trees sorting the sun's rays into highlights, the freshly mown look of the grass, chatty laughter filling the still, sticky air all seemed very Victorian. I half expected a peacock to come strutting onto the canvas. Even the roll of toilet paper in the hand of a woman, slightly unrolled and swaying gracefully in synch with the dresses, looked a part of the scene.

I peed at the side of the road.

Nearing Kamwenge, the country turned to Montana. Wide, grassy plains rose into soft bumps of hills to the east. Flat-topped acacia trees dotted the land. To the west, a road led to Queen Elizabeth National Park where elephants and hippos and lions roam free and the snow-capped Rwenzori Mountains scribe the western edge of Uganda. The van lurched and I banged my head on the window. "Sorry," John said. Another sneaky pothole. Tightening my grip on the hand-hold, I was still captivated by the scenery. Breathtaking views. Perfect weather. There were few people. Someday there will be eco-lodges here.

The road flattened and we entered Kamwenge town which I imagined looked like a crossroads village in pre-war Montana. Where five minutes ago we saw no people, we seem to

have found everyone talking, carrying, hauling, kids in uniforms with school books, ladies with baskets on their heads.
We stopped for petrol. A bored young man in army green was
squishing ants with the muzzle of his gun. He looked up and
wandered over to the van asking if we had an extra bottle of
water.

"Do you have bullets in that gun?" I asked.

"Yes, of course." he said, waving it around. "What good
would it be if there were no bullets?"

"Are you guarding the gasoline?"

"Yes," he replied. "In case someone drives off without
paying."

"You would shoot him?"

"Yes," he said, smiling. I gave him a bottle of water.

Once again underway, we bumped across a railroad crossing. "John, this is the railroad you were telling me about?"

"Yes, Mzee. We have a railroad."

The X-shaped railroad crossing signs were there, barely
clinging to their last chips of black and white paint. The only
rails I could see were the ones we just drove across because
there were none as far as the eye could see in either direction.

"John, where are the rails?"

"They are coming," he said. "I think a private concern is
planning to put them back."

"Where will it go?"

"All the way to Kampala."

"You will need it if these people begin farming cash crops."

"Yes?"

"Yes," I thought, "because if a truck has to use this road,
the produce will be bruised and broken before it gets half way
to market. Kind of like the people in this van."

"Oh," he smiled. "You are right." This is a typical African response to a foreigner's attempt to make light of such dire needs. Polite. Patient. Non-judgmental. And clearly saying, "I get the joke but it's not funny or helpful. Think of something funny or helpful. We need both of those things."

We passed a giant yellow road grader sitting by the side of the road. "John, there is the solution to the roads. Why is it not working (wukking)."

"I am not sure, Mzee," he said. Perhaps they have run out of fuel. Or sometimes the blade is broken and they cannot afford to replace it."

"Oh," I said, shaking my head.

I later related this story to Ben who said, "The roads are maintained by the government. And what probably happened is the driver of the road grader worked a day or so to do what the government wanted, which was just enough to make the town governor happy. Then he drained off the diesel fuel to sell to villagers and then spent the next few days at the local bar.

"It's a problem when the government does these things," he added. If there was a private company maintaining the roads, we would have better roads and no idle road graders. It would be a matter of convincing the government to pay the contractor instead of the road workers. The government wants infrastructure, but they also want people employed. Clearly, we need to train up someone to see that this is an opportunity."

I said, "John, I like the idea of the railroad. It could bring tourists from the East to here and the national park. And it could take people and goods from here to market."

"I like that idea too," he said, not chuckling.

Through town, past a shacky neighborhood, a road to the right through tall grass and a turnoff through a copse of osier bushes stood the school. "In February, we will have our first classes," John said. I believed him. Here was a brick building with wrought iron window guards in place, roof on, waiting for interior finishes. A latrine 20 feet deep and sculpted perfectly square yawned to the sky, waiting for an outbuilding and a century of deposits. The mango tree was bearing fruit. A pile of bricks had been made for future building. Clusters of children had appeared from the bush and stood watching in their ghostly way.

"This is our dream," John said. "If we can teach these people useful skills, they will not be poor and needy for long. I wanted you to see it, Mzee."

"I salute your heart and your commitment, John."

He shrugged off the comment with "It simply has to be done."

The road back seemed shorter. Perhaps all the jostling and bottomings out and the evasive maneuvers had become normal and, if so, we had become more accepting of the situation we were in. Which is what the people of Kamwenge had done. This is life. The road is bad. Deal with it. We had finally learned this and somehow we felt less foreign.

The late afternoon sun turned the dust redder, the tree bathroom cozier. Soon we were back in Mbarara. The van looked like it had just finished the Dakar Rallye and my shoulders ached from hanging on to the crash bar all day. John said he would be going back later that week. Dedication is like that. I went to take a nap.

Six months later I again traveled the road to Kamwenge to see John's Secondary School and Vocational Institute. In the time that had elapsed since my first visit, the road grad-ers had been busy smoothing out the ruts and the gullies. If I had expected another road massage, there would be none today. The rails that had been visible at the railroad crossing in Kamwenge Town had been buried by the road machines. The crossing sign had lost more paint. We passed a white, one-story stucco building, John said, "Mzee, that is your accommodation for tonight. It is a new guest house." Really, a new guest house?

The improved road ended shortly after we passed through the town. I would not miss my massage after all. The country had not changed; it was lush and green, bursting with unculti-vated vigor. The people had not changed: men toiled in small enterprises operating out of mud-and-stick huts, women with pots and bundles on their heads strode through the Wild West towns while men watched from in front of the saloon, children passing time sitting in the dirt or watching with wide eyes as a van of *Mzungus* whizzed by.

I didn't expect much when we pulled past the thicket that marked the entrance to the school, but I was dumbfounded at what I saw. Students playing volleyball. Students in the class-rooms. A foundation being dug to build more classrooms. A house for teachers nearly completed. A pole building being used as a vocational training center. An eight-stall latrine building built over the enormous hole in the ground. I could not hide my surprise. "John, this is amazing. Where has it all come from?"

"I told you, Mzee. We would open the school in February. It is now June. We have 82 students and eight faculty includ-ing a headmaster. We use local materials and local laborers. They will build as fast as we can come up with money."

"So the school fees paid by students cover the teacher salaries?"

"Well, no, not yet. Many of the parents cannot afford school fees. The teachers are working for no salary right now. We will have to pay them soon, but we are still waiting for funds. I think we will ask people to sponsor kids in this school and use that money to cover salaries."

"Don't you think the teachers will get tired of working for no salary?"

"Eventually, yes, maybe," John said. "But they are young, mostly recent graduates from teacher colleges looking for experience. Some of the faculty receives money from Christian organizations that also use their services. For now everyone is enthusiastic about the project. We will most likely have to pay them some day."

I had to ask. "John, I've known you for some time and I know you receive support for your ministry but I know it is not a great deal of money. This is a big project. How are you able to pay for it all?"

"You know, Mzee, Jolly and I are committed to making this school a success," he replied. "The hardest part was starting the project. Now that it is up and running and we see the progress people are making in a short amount of time, we are convinced this is how God wants us to spend our lives and our resources. We receive a certain amount of money for family support from our main ministry. Jolly and I are spending half of that family support money on building this school. You know I have six children with one in university, three in boarding school and two still at home. We have made this a family project. We are not suffering and if we do, the people that come out of this school will make it worth it. I have complete faith that God will find the funds for us to succeed. After all, this is His project. We are only Noah and his wife, building an ark to save a lost generation of people."

My American mind was having a hard time processing this project and the attitude behind it. If I were going to build a school, I would have cash in the bank and a mortgage lined up along with a business plan that outlined how I would pay off the loan. I would only start digging and building walls when the funding was set, a number of students had committed to tuition with cash deposits. *But God was not included as a partner in my plan as He was in John's.* There was no faith, only numbers and contingencies. Could I get people to work for me for free? I doubt it. Could I build buildings, attract 82 eager students and a faculty to teach them in a few months? I doubt it. Once again, the African way has opened my eyes and a little voice inside told me to seriously pay attention to what I am seeing.

"Come, Mzee, let me show you where our future students will come from," John said. We got back in the van and traveled a mile or so down the dusty road to the local primary school. The children were all in class working the small farm plot with hand tools. As we walked the grounds to go find them, we noticed a sign on every tree: "Delay Sex." "Stay Virgin." "Abstain from Sex." "AIDS kills." The President's drumbeat message from the eighties was still being pounded out.

Behind the classroom building several acres of tilled ground sat baking in the sun. A cluster of girls in bright blue dress uniforms worked one corner. A cluster of boys in matching blue shirts wielded mattocks to till the soil nearby. "These children learn farming in school because that is what people do around here," John said. "Imagine what would happen if we organized sizeable plots – 10 or 20 acres – to plant coffee or maize or spices or beans or tree seedlings – and then took the education these children are getting and trained them with advanced knowledge in farming techniques, business, product development, management – and they became the people who build enterprises that employ people and make money for their village. That is what we are trying to do. These kids are our future." When John introduced us as missionaries from America, they grew silent, but we could see questions forming in their minds.

At last, one of the young men spoke to the nearest *Mzungu*: "Mzee, would you like to try digging?"

"I would," the man said and grabbed the heavy hoe. He worked mightily hacking at the soil, doing about a 50% job. The students smiled and snickered.

"Do you dig in America?" the student asked.

"No," the visitor replied.

"Then how do you eat?" the student asked.

"There are people who are farmers in America," the visitor explained. "They till the earth with machines and grow enough food for everyone."

"Everyone?" the young son of subsistence farmers stopped hoeing. He was trying to imagine what he had just heard. There was no way he could understand that a country with fewer farmers than Uganda could feed a nation 14 times larger than this place and have plenty left over to export and also pay farmers not to farm because the surpluses would be too high. "Hmm," he said and went back to work.

"John," I asked. When you teach vocations, where will the trained people work?"

"We are not sure, Mzee. Maybe here. Maybe the city. Somewhere. God will give us the skills and the work."

# PART IV:

## Journal Notes

*"Difficult times have helped me to understand better than before, how infinitely rich and beautiful life is in every way, and that so many things that one goes worrying about are of no importance whatsoever."*

-<u>Isak Dinesen</u>, *Author, Out of Africa*

# All Who Roam
# Are Not Lost

*"I soon realized that no journey carries one far unless, as it extends into the world around us, it goes an equal distance into the world within."*
-Lillian Smith, author *Strange Fruit*

In the craft villages, you can find many images of the ideal Ugandan woman. She appears drawn on batik, in paintings, in carvings, crudely wood-burned onto pale wood slats, and even in charcoal on back-street walls. She is tall and thin and slightly pregnant. She strides perfectly erect with a basket on her head, a baby strapped to her back, a mattock for working the soil in one hand and a basket with water and food in the other. The images do not do the Ugandan woman justice.

From the time they are little girls, Ugandan women are driven to be the worker bees of society. All girls learn to balance loads on their head... baskets of grain or water or laundry, bundles of sticks, bales of cloth, loads of potato plants. In the city, it is common to see a gaggle of girls in their school uniforms walking home balancing school books on their heads. It is a wonder to me that, even carrying loads of 40 or 50 pounds every day, year after year, people do not seem to suffer from neck pain.

From the time they are very young, Ugandan women learn to bend from the waist with straight legs when they work in the fields, do laundry, cook over fires or pick children from the floor. They do not bend or squat to work and they do not work on their knees. They bend in half. Somehow this posture allows them to toil in the fields all day, turning the soil or harvesting crops and, at the end of the day, carry burdens home on their heads never showing fatigue. Even the grandmas in the rural areas who think nothing of walking five or ten miles barefoot up and down steep hills, seem to remain flexible well into their seventies and eighties.

When we were building the Kishanje Learning Advancement Center, the earth moving crew was a phalanx of 15 women with mattocks. The first team of five would loosen and move the soil, the second team would move the next layer of soil and the third would grade the parcel. It took a full day and 15 people to do the work one man on a Bobcat... if there was one within 1,000 miles... could do in an hour. Women brought bricks to the masons two at a time atop their heads, walking through the construction site in bare feet. More than a million bricks went into the project. Walking down a 500-foot hill to a stream, the women filled five-gallon jerry cans and carried them on their heads, a 40-pound load, up the hill in order to have water to mix the mortar. They laughed and joked the whole way working dawn to dusk.

I inadvertently came upon a young man one day as he was deep in prayer. He looked up when I walked into the room and I apologized for the interruption. He said, "No problem. I was just sending a knee-mail to God."

I love Uganda's largest daily newspaper, the *New Vision*. If it is true that a country is free when there is freedom of the press, then Uganda is one of the freest societies on earth. At a newsstand in Kampala which might in fact be a woman selling papers from a blanket on the sidewalk, one can choose from no less than eight daily news publications. *New Vision* is the largest. Some think it is the President's personal news medium because he is on the cover so often, but I don't see it. His Excellency is not extolled in every article and he receives regular candid advice from the Op-Ed pages. In fact, the older he gets, the more criticism he receives.

What is refreshing about *New Vision* is that there is little Western wire service content. In the U.S., the press services consolidate news items and distribute to their members. Editors then take the supplied materials to fill the space between the ads. That is why you will most likely read the same story in a newspaper in Denver, Chicago, or Knoxville and hear the same bits on television and radio on any given day. It has been several decades since a newspaper in the U.S. relied solely on its own editorial staff for its content. Yet that is what we find in Uganda today.

Page one *New Vision* will describe Besigye, a candidate running for President as a "wild-eyed leper" or blare "Man-Eating Crocodile Shot Dead." Page three will feature a photo of an enormous, gnarled tree with a caption about people who live in its roots and believe the tree is their God. Page five will have a story chastising husbands who may be thinking about straying away... zero grazing it will say with the column next door offering advice on lovemaking. One issue featured a headline with type four inches tall quoting the President: "Kill Kony," referring to a fanatical rebel in the north.

The news is fresh. It is original. A little sensational but still interesting. The paper comes stapled together so people can't sneak a peek. It's everything a newspaper should be, all for just 1,500 shillings a day.

When asked if the missionary house in Kishanje Village has running water, Dr. Ben answered, "In fact, we do. The women run down the hill with a jerry can, fill it in the stream and run it back up the hill for you to use."

Every time I go to Uganda, I wonder "Where are the Americans?"

It's not white faces I seek. There are plenty of white-skinned preachers and missionaries, government people and aid workers. But where are the business people? This country is bursting with opportunity, with low inflation and a work-force that includes highly educated people, people used to hard, physical work and thousands starving for work of any kind. The government pleads for foreign investment, yet the only established American enterprises I find are Citibank, Pepsi and Coca Cola. Even the Texas Cowboy Grill is owned by a man from Lebanon. American-made products are around but American-led production is not. Most products are from China.

In 2005, I asked the United States Ambassador to Uganda Jimmy Kolker why there didn't seem to be an American busi-ness presence here. "Uganda needs foreign investment," he said. "But it is hard to do business here. Electricity costs are about the highest in the world and the supply is erratic. Trans-portation is difficult. At the same time, Uganda has great resources: an educated population, low labor costs, and good telecom infrastructure which make it a good place for call centers such as those found in India and Ghana. The agricultural environment makes this an ideal place for growing and processing food products and ingredients.

"You may not see them, but there are some American enterprises here," he added. "A Kansas firm recently invested $1 million in a flour mill. Nearly all the vanilla extract we buy in the U.S. comes from Uganda... that's a new development, an export of more than $20 million. They are also exporting fish – tilapia – to the U.S. and garments. I think Target stores have been buying apparel made in Uganda. These are all good, but they are not the big American investment breakthrough the leadership would like to see."

Former Ambassador Kolker is correct: doing business in Uganda has its challenges. Electrical supply is expensive and erratic. As a land-locked nation, fuel and shipping are dependent on conditions in Kenya. Petrol and diesel are expensive. At the same time, the pioneers who tamed the American West endured harsh weather, Indian attacks, locusts and God knows what else in order to prosper. If we think of Uganda as just a different frontier, what's the problem?

Transportation costs and erratic electricity didn't prevent eager entrepreneurs from staking claims at Sutter's Mill or the Klondike. There were no guarantees of success for pioneer families during the Kansas Land Rush. The Goulds and Vanderbilts didn't worry about infrastructure – they created it by building railroads. When Philip D. Armour wanted to ship meat from the Chicago stock yards to New York consumers he invented the refrigerated rail car, the meat kept cold with ice cut out of lakes in Wisconsin. Where is this pioneering spirit in venturing into Uganda?

Americans could make fortunes with world class expertise in fast food, building railroads, growing corn and beans with high yields. What about manufacturing and distribution of dairy products, building tractors, fixing copy machines? Doesn't someone want to produce indigenous-artist pop music in a region where 75% of the population is under 25 years old? What about running eco-lodges in a nation filled with natural wonders? Isn't there a food importer that wants to bring to the tables in Europe and America the luscious fruits and vegetables grown in this garden of a country? Billions are waiting to be made in the manufacturing of high-efficiency solar panels and solar roofing material in a vast market lying on the equator. Enormous tracts of land are available for agriculture in a region being held hostage by fuel prices; think biofuel. Does anyone have the guts and patience to bring organization, management skills and proven best practices to a place that desperately needs and wants these things? Other nations are already here; will America be left behind?

As Ben Tumuheirwe said, "With our history of higher education and Christian work ethic, Uganda has always been a producer of leaders for Africa. Many nations in sub-Saharan Africa are working to replace its 'lost generation,' the millions who died of AIDS and there has never been a time when leadership has been more in demand. When the kids we are teaching today become adept at engineering, commerce, manufacturing, management, agriculture and politics, they will have influence in every nation on the continent. We must give them modern 'can do' attitudes. We must equip them to achieve great things. We must teach them to dream and take care of themselves and their families. And we must have productive enterprises here where they may use their expertise. Only then will we have peace and prosperity on this continent.

"Yet, to do so," he emphasized, "We need people from the first world to invest in us, to trust us, to teach us. We invite you to come make money with us. Welcome us into the world economy. We will welcome you with radiant smiles and hot tea and open arms."

So, I wonder, where *are* the Americans in this new land of opportunity?

In the U.S., we ask "where do you live?" In Uganda, people ask each other, "Where do you stay?"

We have said it before, there are children everywhere in Uganda. Nearly every other woman seems to be holding a baby. The schools are so full of children, the rooms are not big enough to hold them. I wondered, how in the world will Uganda and Africa support so many children in the days to come?

"The question you are asking," Dr. Ben said, "is how do we control overpopulation, yes?"

"Yes," I replied. "It seems impossible."

"It can be done," he said. "The answer is education, education, education. You have seen kids come up through our schools with big goals, a focus on career. You have seen the graduates deep in their work and not thinking about having children, happy to be contributing to society. They are satisfied with that. If people do not have such goals and they are not equipped to reach beyond an impoverished life, the only way they can feel significant is to have children."

Ben's words rang in my ears as I went to All Saints Cathedral in Kampala in 2011. Attending the four services there were thousands of what could be called Uganda's middle class families. Instead of nine, ten or eleven kids per family as I counted in the rural village, here families had two or three kids per family. I hoped this was a trend... that, with education, people were having children later and having fewer of them. I was seeing it for myself and once again admired Ugandans for attacking a major social issue in a highly pragmatic way. But if education doesn't work fast enough, perhaps the government should give every rural family a television programmed only with late-night talk shows. That'd do it.

First worlders see a baby lamb or bunny, a chicken or a goat and they want to hold it, cuddle it, play with it. The local people look on with question marks on their faces that say, "why do you play with your food?"

In the West, we see the hand of God in times of peril – floods, wars, fires and hurricanes. It is then that people's faith takes a physical form as they become instruments for God and begin to help their neighbors. When we (in the West) are not having disasters or personal crises, however, God often returns to His former role of a Sunday morning afterthought. God is more visible at All Saints Cathedral in Kampala where very comfortable middle class people come faithfully to worship and pack four services on Sunday morning. These people remember the perils, the bad times. They sing, they pray, they return to their homes and on Monday, return to their busy lives. A few hours away in the still-rural environs, worship happens on a whole new level, where people meet not to fulfill a Sunday obligation but to glorify God as a group expression of what they have been doing as individuals and families all week. These are people who depend on God every day for their very existence because every day could be their last, but they greet every day is a joy. They are openly, enthusiastically grateful to their *Tata Ruhanga*, Father God, and are anxious to tell their creator and provider of life just how much He means to them.

Worship in the city might last two hours. Up country, it may be three and seem much shorter. Worship in the city will have a choir in bright robes singing into microphones to the accompaniment of an electric piano. Up country, the church will have three robeless choirs with an entire congregation singing and dancing to the accompaniment of one drum. Worship in the city will have velvet bags passed down the aisles for collection. Up country, people come forward with coins, poultry or produce and smiles on their faces to fill the collection basket. In the city, people walk quietly out of church, get in their cars and inch their ways through the molasses of traffic to get home. Up country, people dance out of church. They hang around, greeting one another and then wander off down the road or various paths in groups, laughing and chatting as they go.

I recall walking out of the rural church at Kagyera exhausted after a half day's worship. I was with another American, a strong Iowa Christian in his seventies. He shook his head and turned to me with a wry smile on his face. "Now THAT's what I call church," he said.

I was surprised to see an enormous photo on the front page of the *New Vision* daily newspaper with President Yoweri

Kaguta Museveni walking proudly with the Aga Khan down
the steps of the newly renovated five-star Serena Hotel. The
Aga Khan is the hereditary spiritual leader of a sect of Islam
that represents some 15 million Muslims. The investment is
Muslim. The employees of the new Serena Hotel are Muslim. He was quoted as saying, "We see so much opportunity
here, we are immediately beginning plans to build eco-lodges
throughout the country." Guess who will work in those facilities. Muslims.

For those who see a Christian vs. Muslim competition
playing on the world stage, the developments in Uganda are
disturbing because the Muslim agenda is simple: we will rule
the world. And Muslim leaders are patient. They are unflag-
ging in their mission and they are well-funded. I could not
help but recall a conversation with the leader of the largest evangelical church in Cairo Egypt who said: "There is a
strategy for establishing Muslim presence in the third world
that has worked without modification for more than a hundred years. It is this: show poor people that being Muslim
brings wealth and security. Here's how it works: A business
is started in a rural town. Locals are hired. They are paid
above average. The owners make it clear they are Muslim
and, if the workers also become Muslim, they will earn more
money. The workers agree. Soon a Muslim school opens in
the town. Then a mosque. The workers' neighbors witness
the newfound prosperity in their peers and ask, "How did
you do it?" The reply? "I became a Muslim." Soon, the town
is a Muslim town led by an Imam or a Caliph who becomes
the spiritual / economic / social / economic leader of the
town – in essence, running the place exclusive of any non-
Muslim. It is way of Islam.

While Muslim populations and influence continue to change the face of what the late journalist Oriana Fallaci called "Eurabia," the same scenario is being repeated in hundreds of towns in Uganda. It is happening on a large scale in the capital city of Kampala where in October of 2006, Moammar Qadaffi completed a $2 billion project that includes a lavish new mosque along with a 150-shop commercial center, a 200-bed hospital and a university on the top of Old Kampala hill in the capital.[51] It is said to be the largest mosque in Africa with 15 entrances to admit 5,000 worshipers at a time. People who have seen it – infidels are barred from visiting – say the mosaics and carving and gold gilt walls are stunning. It is all intended to impress worshipers who want some of that wealth for themselves and will obey anyone who can give it to them. The university offers free education to students who are Muslim; the stores offer low-cost goods to Muslims.

Contrast this with the many Christian leaders in Uganda who are eager to tell young people that Jesus is the answer and that God will provide, but neglect to tell them how. These are nothing but hollow words if the people God has already blessed do not share their secrets of earthly success with the newly blessed. God's promise and Jesus' words must have tangible economic truth behind them because what this country – and every country in Africa needs in order to become self-sustaining is enterprise. In 2007, it was announced that The Bill and Melinda Gates Foundation had pledged $750 million for Uganda to investigate ways to upgrade the nation's telecommunications infrastructure. That is good news, but better news would be for Microsoft to set up a programming and service center that employs and inspires people.

---

51   http://www.newvision.co.ug/D/8/12/528225/National%20Mosque

If Christians don't provide the capital and the expertise, the Muslims will. They already are. The very spiritual future of free and productive Africa is at stake.

I awoke one morning to find a break in the schedule and thus, with no pressing business and without hesitation or remorse, decided to go find some lions... a real safari, the real Africa. Missionary Matt and his wife would be our guides. It was a short two-hour drive from Mbarara to Queen Elizabeth National Park where lions, cheetahs, elephants, cranes, hippos, kobs and other creatures live abundantly. We stopped to buy bananas, the standard driving snack and marveled at the tea plantations that covered the hills like thick green velvet. It was clear we were getting near the main gate when clusters of baboons appeared by the side of the road looking cute with dour faces and pink butts and expecting a banana just because.

Once inside the park, the savannah stretched to the horizon with grass as tall as the car. Any animal intent on ambush would have it easy here because no one would see them coming. We drove for an hour, then two, farther and farther into the deepest reaches of the park looking for lions. "They are here," Missionary Matt said. "I can feel them." Sure enough, we rounded a corner to find two female lions sunning themselves on a rock in an open space. They took little notice of us until we opened our doors. Then one mother sauntered purposefully toward us. We closed the doors. She lay flat in the grass, staring, when suddenly two cubs scampered out of a clump of bushes next to our car and ran to her for protection. She fed them, licked them and batted them about and then walked back to her rock for a nap. What a sight.

That evening, we sat on the terrace of Mweya Lodge, a multi-star resort built high on a bluff overlooking the Lake Edward channel, a panorama of green foothills and the snow-capped Rwenzori Mountains in the distance. The African Camp-style building made of varnished logs, stone and glass is surrounded by lush gardens. It is as though we are on a different planet from where we have recently been. The bar features a two-story rock fireplace flanked by elephant tusks. The dining room is an open terrace of white tablecloths, candles and glinting silver in twilight where guests dine on fine cuisine and vintage wine. Small birds flit through the lobby.

It was my pleasure to offer our young American missionaries a night in this place as they had been in Uganda for nearly a year building a home, learning the language and wrestling with local customs, all on a shoestring budget. They needed a break. And, well, I had always wanted to stay at Mweya.

The night was warm and still. Comfortable social tourist laughter riffled around us to the tinkling of ice in drinks. We marveled at our luck at finding a mother lion and her cubs when something caught my eye. I turned my head to see, not more than 30 feet away, a large, wet, gray hippopotamus munching on the lawn. Apparently it had scaled forty feet of river bank and stopped by for a visit. The other tourists soon saw it as well and moved quickly to the short railing that separated us from this large bit of nature. As we watched, it sauntered closer and, then ten feet away, worked its way around the front of the terrace. The beast was the size of a Honda Civic. Its little pig eyes stared straight ahead. Then it turned and, like a delivery van, backed up to the railing at the edge of the terrace and... crapped on us. I can now attest with the authority of an eye witness that, when a hippo poops, it doesn't just drop its load, no siree. A hippo projects its package from the rear gun and switches its tail rapidly to disperse the debris... very much like the old phrase of the sh— hitting the fan. The tourists scattered. And when it was finished, the hippo continued its meander around the building, ultimately disappearing back down the river bank.

We laughed out loud and returned to our table which was now spattered with hippo poop. The young missionary wife picked up her glass with a brown glob stuck to it and said calmly, "I believe I'll get another glass."

One of my favorite American missionaries from Texas has a sign over her porcelain hole in the bathroom floor that states, "Don't squat with your spurs on."

After being in Uganda, I've noticed that with automation, human capacity seems to diminish and, ultimately disappear. For example: I realized that using a word processor for decades has resulted in a decline in the quality and skill of my own handwriting. Likewise, the written word and reading seem to cause a decline in reliance and quality of memory. Vehicles cause a decline in the need for physical activity such as walking or hauling. Dishwashers cause a decline in family chores & working together over the sink. Kids in the Twitter Age have a hard time remembering things. This is not an indictment of mechanization, automation or modern society, but is merely an observation that's made clear when we watch people who are not exposed to these modern day things exhibiting inspiring traits and qualities of human skills rarely seen today in the western world.

One night after showing the Jesus film ran late into the night, we gave a young girl a ride. We let her off at a break in the woods, a path that apparently led to her home. The track was steep, the night inky black and she was barefoot but without hesitation, she scampered away, her eyes used to the dark and her feet knowing exactly where to go.

What about simple communication? In rural Kishanje Village, if you need to get a message to someone, you pull a young boy aside and give him a message on a piece of paper or you simply tell him your message. Somehow he knows where to find the recipient and deliver the message. You get the sense that everyone knows where everyone else is at any given moment in time, a foreign concept to those of us who would be lost in such a task without the use of telephone, email, GPS or scribbled notes left on the refrigerator door.

In the new century, we have become conditioned to not really need to know where people are, just that they can be reached. I may be in my office or on assignment ten states away, but my daughter can call on her cell phone to gush about how her team won a big soccer game. That is one of the blessings of the modern age. At the same time, when I am in the far-off hills of Kishanje, I suspect that such immediate news has dulled our sense of community. I would love for a small boy to run up to me as I'm working and say, "Mzee, Uncle Herbert would like to invite you to a meal this evening. What is your answer?" I would say: "Please tell Uncle Herbert I accept with pleasure. Thank you, Bernard." I would give him a fresh carrot and send him on his way. It is a small thing, but when I experience it, I feel closer to my fellow human beings and that I am a tangible component in the community fabric. I am real, recognized as necessary. Someone knows where to find me no matter where I am. And in the process, I have been able to show another human being that they too have value;

I have a chance to share my blessings with him, to show kindness, share a smile, shake a hand, pat a shoulder, gently kick a pair of buttocks as they run from my house. I can discern the urgency of the message by the look on the face of the messenger. This just doesn't happen with a cell phone.

If the news of my daughter's soccer victory had to wait until I returned home, the news would certainly be less spontaneous, but it would necessarily need to be stored in that place of her mind where she keeps the things she must tell Dad when he gets home. In that place is anticipation, a looking forward to sharing, an eagerness to see Dad in order to bring him up to date. In this scenario, Dad has value beyond being the guy who answers the phone. At the same time, Dad looks forward to returning home to hear the news of the day from each family member. It gives everyone a reason to sit down to a meal together. Dad has the chance to be an affirmer, a motivator, a repository of joys and fears of the family, and also a voice of perspective, the dispenser of wisdom. This is the role of the hunter who, gone for days or weeks at a time in pursuit of food for the family, returns with the life-sustaining fruits of his labor and the family feels secure.

I enjoy the scientific gadgetry, the conveniences and the advance of technology. But, seeing how the iPhone consumes its users playing Angry Birds in contrast to people who have never been exposed to such things or the technology leading up to them, I can only imagine what blithering idiots we will be 50 years from now.

I miss seeing ant hills taller than children and the children playing on them.

I wanted to know about poverty in Africa so I went to the expert, Dr. Augustus Nuwagaba, a Professor at Makerere University and also a busy consultant. His specialty is poverty which in Africa is a lucrative niche for a consultant. Business is good. Dr. Augustus has four houses, his own office building and drives a Pajero. He has the President's ear.

"Poverty... what is poverty?" he mused. "It is not living with dirt floors or mud walls or living without hot water. It is being stuck in a life where you cannot get enough good food or send your children to school, where one generation leaves nothing for the next generation to build on."

"And so," I asked, "what is the solution to poverty?"

He replied simply: "It is people working hard with their own hands in order to make not only their lives better, but those of their neighbors as well. And that means becoming economically self-sufficient. Growing more crops than are necessary to feed the family and selling the surplus at market. Manufacturing things for sale. Offering value-added services for money. These things require knowledge, experience and skills... and a political environment that allows such things because, if people earn money for their labor, the result is self-sufficiency, personal and community strength and security for the family.

"In pre-Colonial days," he explained, "the people throughout the Great Lakes Region and in many other parts of Africa did these things, albeit in a different context. The village worked together. People took care of each other. Villages, tribes and kingdoms traded with one another or squabbled with each other.

"Then came the Colonial era which showed how abundant this country, this region, this continent could be in providing goods to a world market. But things fell into disarray with independence as the Colonials left very little expertise behind. Dictators stepped in and stripped the life out of countries for their own gain. And then as you know disease ravaged our society. Today we have learned much and our economy – our standard of life is growing."

He elaborated: "We have massive tea plantations where people labor year round. We have sugar cane fields and processing plants. We grow tobacco. We export tens of thousands of metric tons of bananas and, most recently, vanilla, spices, coffee... very good coffee... and fruit crops. All of these operations are privately owned, primarily by foreign companies or foreign nationals. I am not complaining. This is good because many people are earning money and feeding their families. But if we are to alleviate poverty in Uganda, we need to have profitable enterprises owned by Ugandans where the village spirit... the sense of caring and sharing of skills will benefit entire generations of people.

"And we need people to buy our goods," he said. "Many current researchers have proven that massive aid from the West has caused more harm than good in that it has created generations of people dependent on aid and not on their own labor or ingenuity. Even well-meaning Christian NGOs supplying clothes and school supplies and mosquito nets from abroad... why? We make those things here... buy them here. Instead of planting another church, plant a shop or a crop or a way to manufacture things. Give us expertise, not castoff clothing. We don't need a hand out, we need a hand up. We don't need gifts or grants; we need customers. That will end the cycle of poverty. With economic independence, health levels will rise, family size will lessen and Uganda will become an even bigger market for world goods. Then we will be poor no more."

My hosts and I were stopped on the road one morning by the tax collectors. It was a roadblock of sorts where men in green army uniforms lay steel tire spikes in the road to make sure traffic would stop. When it was our turn, a tax man asked to see the driver's license. On that license was a sticker that verified that the man's taxes had been paid.

"How do they know you have paid the proper tax," I asked.

"Oh, the driver replied, we are taxed by our job title so the job title on the driver's license matches a code on the sticker," he replied. After a brief glance at the license, the man in green moved the spikes and we went on our way.

At the Kamwenge Guest House in rural Southwest Uganda we were delighted to find a fairly new structure with large rooms, each with a clean, tiled bathroom complete with flush toilet and shower wand. There were even knobs for hot and cold water.

The first night we stayed there, everything operated as expected. The toilet flushed once. Shower water came on demand, though reluctantly, from the cold spigot only. Clearly the hot water faucet was a promise of things to come. This was no problem because there was the ubiquitous plastic basin ready with water for toilet flushing, water for bathing and a small jug of hot water delivered to the room in the morning. The second night, the toilet flushed but did not refill. The shower trickled.

"It is a matter that the water tank is not full," the jittery manager in Muslim cap and long shirt explained. In the morning, however, I understood the real problem. In back of the guest house, sitting on a concrete platform was a 20,000-liter plastic tank. Pipes ran from the bottom of the tank through the guest house wall, fulfilling the needs of its guests by gravity. The tank was replenished by a pipe which ran from gutters on the roof to the top of the tank whenever it rained. But it hadn't rained in a week. So this morning, two pickup trucks had been dispatched to a tap in town where water from the mountains is caught in a small reservoir. There, a crew of six men filled dozens, maybe hundreds of five-gallon jerry cans with water, drove them back to the guest house and lifted them 15 feet up a home-made ladder to dump into the tank.

As I was watching, fascinated at the enormous amount of labor being spent to provide water for guests five gallons at a time, I overheard a conversation in the hallway behind me. The voice was American. Female.

"This is the second morning in row we have had no hot water in our room," it said with great indignity.

"It is a matter that the water tank is not full," the manager said. "We should have the problem corrected soon."

"Well, I certainly hope you do," the voice said with Colonial authority.

I wished that guest would go round back of the building to see what it took to make water come out of her tap.

I was heading home after a month in Uganda. On my second eight-hour flight in as many days, we were on final approach to Chicago and I was hurrying to finish Joseph Conrad's *Heart of Darkness*. In the book, Marlow has at last returned to the nation's capital after his grueling Congo River adventure as a white European man in the untamed African wilderness. He reflects:

*"I found myself back in the sepulchral city resenting the sight of people hurrying through the streets to filch a little money from each other, to devour their infamous cookery, to gulp their unwholesome beer, to dream their insignificant and silly dreams. They trespassed upon my thoughts. They were intruders whose knowledge of life was to me an irritating pretence, because I felt so sure they could not possibly know the things I knew. Their bearing, which was simply the bearing of commonplace individuals going about their business in the assurance of perfect safety was offensive to me alike the outrageous flauntings of folly in the face of a danger it is unable to comprehend. I had no particular desire to enlighten them, but I had some difficulty in restraining myself from laughing in their faces so full of stupid importance."*

I realized then that Uganda is my spiritual battery. I go there to plug in, to immerse myself in a culture that depends on God, His blessings and the teachings of His son, Jesus Christ. Touching the lives of people there energizes me. When my battery is full to bursting, I return home, somewhat aglow, ready to tell people what I have seen. I will talk to anyone who will listen. But no matter how enthusiastic I am, no matter how many stories I tell, no matter how many photos I share, people do not share my spark.

It's not their fault. They can't know that the red dust of Africa is magic growing powder for the soul. They haven't heard a symphony of heavenly harmonic voices accompanied only by a goatskin drum. They haven't prayed with people who find so much joy in worship they must raise their hands to heaven and leap off the ground in faithful fervor. I have become a stranger in my own land because, like Marlowe, I have been touched by something most of my countrymen will never know... unless they go.

Current Information:

The stories in this book were accumulated over more than eight years. Here is a brief update of some referenced details as of this printing:

1. The real inflation rate in Uganda has grown from 6% in 2006 to 21% due to the skyrocketing cost of fuel and food. Famines in Somalia and Kenya are drawing off the food supply of Uganda which results in higher prices at home.

2. The price of petrol in Kampala at last glance was the equivalent of $8.00 per gallon. The price in Uganda shillings has more than tripled but the dollar has grown nearly twice as much in value per shilling. The net effect of fuel costs is that locally prices have tripled in the last five years. If the exchange rate with the USD was the same today as it was in 2005, gasoline would cost $18.00 per gallon.

3. A entry visa at Entebbe airport now costs $50.00

4. The Mbarara Road has been widened and paved. Now people can drive faster but fatal accidents are fewer.

5. Schools that opened in Kishanje Village in 2008 now enroll more than 350 students and regularly rank in the highest percentile of schools nationwide based on standardized testing.

6. The people have not changed. Their hospitality, sense of humor and reliance on faith endure.

# About the Author:

L ee B. Mulder has been a writer and photographer for more than four decades. Raised in Chicago, he earned a Journalism degree at the University of Wisconsin at Madison. In 1995, Mulder became active in international missions, an avocation that has taken him to Europe, Peru, Mexico, Honduras, Egypt, Ethiopia, Dubai, Burundi, Rwanda and Uganda. He helped found Juna Amagara Ministries www.amagara.org in Uganda, East Africa in 2004 and remains active with the work there. Today he divides his time between his family in Chicago and his family in Uganda. Catch up on the latest stories from Uganda at his blog: http://ugandatoday.typepad.com

Made in the USA
Charleston, SC
19 August 2012